The Sheep-eater Shoshoni Indians dwelling in a wickiup shelter at Yellowstone in their mountain camp on Medicine Creek in eastern Idaho in 1877. - Photo Courtesy of the Smithsonian Institute. The Back cover photo is of the statue of Sacajawea taken at the Idaho State Historical Museum in Boise, Idaho. Neither Lewis and Clark nor Sacajawea were ever photographed on the expedition. Author photo.

D1733462

1

Chief Washakie Statue
Downtown Casper, Wyoming
(Photo Courtesy of Wikimedia)

"THE SNAKE PEOPLE"
THE NORTHERN SHOSHONI INDIANS
A REVISED EDITION of SMOKE SIGNALS & WAGON TRACKS

ROBERT D. BOLEN, B.A.

.

Dedication

To my parents, Ralph and Opal Bolen

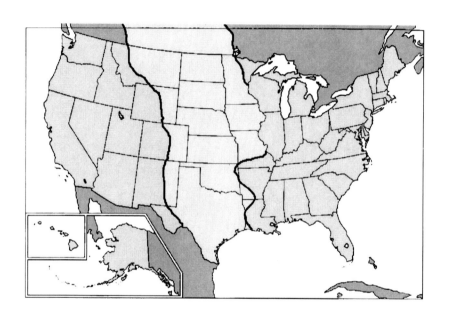

Map of the Great Plains
Courtesy of Wikipedia.org

LIST OF ILLUSTRATIONS

CONTENTS

Sheep-eater Indian Petroglyphs
Photo Courtesy of Wikimedia.org

ACKNOWLEDGEMENTS

My deepest thanks to Teresa, owner of Azusa Publishing, L.L.C., in Denver, Colorado for all of the wonderful iconic Indian post cards she has graciously allowed me to use in this text. The Curtis photos are superb. Pictures really make the book in my estimation. Her ad and website of gorgeous authentic Indian postcards are on page 185. I highly recommend you try the site out.

I have an additional source for photos and thank you so much, Wikimedia, who gave permission for the use of their photos and allowing me the use of their gallery.

Thank you to Bonnie Fitzpatrick, my Graphic Designer for the wonderful job of creating the cover for this work. She does an excellent job.

Thank you to the Library of Congress for the very excellent ancient wickiup photo and thanks to the Smithsonian Institute for the great picture of Washakie's village and the Sheep-eater Indians.

Thanks go out to Ned Eddins, author of "Mountains of Stone," for great photos. I would like to express my gratitude to George and Lise' Jumper for the Appaloosa pix.

Last, but not least, my sincerest thanks to Lightning Source (Ingram Publishing Company) for their professional job of printing this fine publication.

Nez Perce Indian War Chiefs
Photo Courtesy of Wikimedia.org

FOREWORD

Archeologists attest that early man first crossed the Bering Straits over the Arctic Land Bridge from Mongolia onto the continent around 15,000 B.P. in waves after the last Ice Age, and reached American shores. The earliest humans on the continent were the Clovis Man, circa 13,000 years B.P. Nomads lodged in skin tents, moved behind the herds, and hunted bison as they grazed. Some resided in natural caves, lava tubes and rock overhangs. It has been estimated that the Shoshoni arrived around 8,000 B.P. in Canada and were driven southward by stronger tribes, who fought over territory.

These Indians were far ranging from the Eastern Shoshoni to the Northern and Western Shoshoni in present day Idaho from the Great Basin to California and the southwest. Uto-Aztecan speakers made a large language group. The region was carefully chosen by ancestral Shoshoni with a mild climate except in intense summer heat and heavy snowfall. The region was rich with flora, fauna and teemed with buffalo, elk, deer and salmon. Agriculture among the Shoshoni Indians occurred in historic times on the reservation.

East of the Mississippi Indians were defeated in battle, their lands taken from them. They were displaced and removed west of the Mississippi to Indian Territory in Oklahoma. Treaties were signed in the west that took away millions of acres of their land. True, the United States paid for the land at pennies on the dollar and in turn the Indians were placed on their reservations against their will, where the majority remains today, but that is the way of war.

Because of dozens of inquiries about the Shoshoni Indians, the author has taken passages from his previous book, "Smoke Signals & Wagon Tracks," and expounded on it to include the Shoshoni-Bannock American Indian histories in an expanded more completed volume.

11

Salmon River Mountains
Photo Courtesy of Wikipedia.org

CHAPTER ONE
BOISE RIVER SHOSHONI

The Shoshoni were driven out of Canada by fierce Blackfeet and Sioux warriors onto the Plateau, Great Basin and the Great Plains. The Shoshoni Tribe divided into extended family bands west of the Continental Divide and occupied a large portion of western America. Native Americans call themselves "the first people."

Seven tribes of the American Indians dwelled in this region for centuries before the coming of the white man. The Northern Paiute, Bannock and Shoshoni were the southern tribes. Nez Perce, Coeur d'Alene, Kalispell, and Kutenai made up the northern tribes.

In their dialect Shoshoni refer to themselves as "*newe*" or "the people." Shoshone in their tongue means "inland," "in the valley" or "valley people." In time newe was translated as Indian people in general. John Rees, a former Indian Agent at Lemhi Indian Reservation claimed that Shoshoni came from "*Shawnt*" or abundance in their language and Shaw-nip (grass), related much grass for their horses. In the Shoshonean, "taibo" meant white people.

The Shoshoni split into seven bands identified by locations in present day Idaho. There were the Bear River, Boise River (Boise Valley), Bruneau River, Fort Hall (Bannock), Salmon River (Lemhi), Sheep-eater Shoshonis and Eastern Shoshoni of western Wyoming.

The Northern Paiute or *Numa* (the people) and Western Shoshoni lived in the southwest. Western Shoshoni bands named for their dwelling places, Boise, Bruneau, and the Weiser River Shoshoni, who dwelled along the Snake River drainages. The Boise, Payette and Weiser Rivers flow into the Upper Snake River.

13

Plains Antelope
Photo Courtesy of Wikimedia.org

The headwaters of the Boise begin in the Sawtooth Mountains and empties into the Snake River, and Columbia to the Pacific Ocean. The Boise River Shoshonis, (*Win-nes-tahs*) lodged at the mouth of the Boise with cottonwood trees in a shaded peaceful valley, mild weather and cool water

Over time Boise River and Bruneau River Shoshoni intermarried, becoming intermixed as one band. Bannock Indians moved near the Fort Hall Shoshoni and intermarried, becoming the Shoshoni-Bannock people, dwelling near the fur fort. The Bear River Shoshoni lived southeast and the Salmon River (Lemhi) Shoshonis lived north. Sheep-eater Indians lived in the Salmon River Mountains.

The Northern Shoshoni were called the "Snake Indians" by the nearby tribes talking in universal sign language using a slithering hand motion, as "Snake" to demonstrate how quickly that they vanished from sight behind rocks like serpents. The Shoshoni were called "Snakes" because they painted red serpent symbols on sticks that they held in the air in order to frighten their traditional enemies.

No written language existed, but Indians carved elaborate petro-glyphs on caves, rock walls, boulders, and flat stones, especially along streams as "rock art." Symbols of animals, birds, reptiles, warriors, their weapons and geometrics were displayed in stone. Calendars, maps, and murals of hunting and war depicted events. Paint was manufactured from powdered minerals for pigment. They used red ochre. Pigment was mixed with bear grease for fluidity.

They were hunters and gatherers, with division of labor between the sexes: men hunted and fished. The women foraged and gathered, picked berries, dug roots and camas root for flour for bread.

15

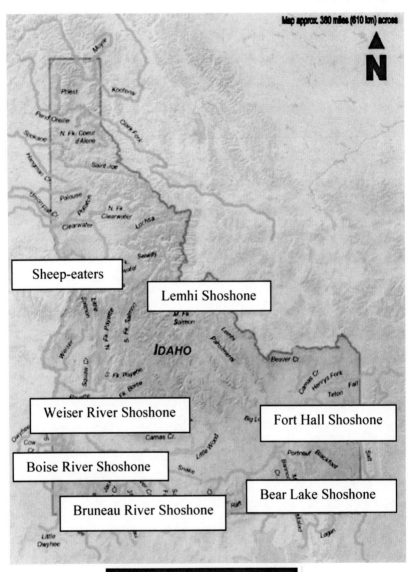

Map approx. 380 miles (610 km) across

N

Sheep-eaters

Lemhi Shoshone

IDAHO

Weiser River Shoshone

Fort Hall Shoshone

Boise River Shoshone

Bear Lake Shoshone

Bruneau River Shoshone

Northern Shoshone Indians

Idaho Photo Map Courtesy of Wikimedia.org

They caught small lizards, rodents, and snakes and moved seasonally to obtain food. Shoshoni women were seen digging roots from the earth. When the Euro-Americans first arrived, the white men called them "Digger Indians."

Indian women were not afraid of work. A mother had duties as a wife and cared for their small children. She worked with her papoose in a cradleboard, strapped on her back. Women cooked, made pottery and baskets.

Buffalo ranged in smaller herds, but grazed in massive herds in the summer mating season. Buffalo were the largest mammal in America. The herds were made up of bulls, cows and calves, like cattle. Buffalo can run speeds up to forty miles per hour.

A bull weighed 2,000 pounds and battled to breed the cows. He would challenge the alpha male to fight. They charged and butted heads together their huge skulls making the impact. Some battled to the death. The victor would mate with the estrus females in the herd.

Wild buffalo roamed free on the Snake River Plain as far west as the Blue Mountains, in America, Canada and Mexico. It was estimated that there were millions of buffalo on the Plains.

The buffalo was Indians' main source of meat to feed their families. A conservative estimation was 3,000,000 buffalo on the American Plains in 1860. Bison fed on grasses, sedges, berries and lichen and used their head to clear the snow.

Before the horse, the band chief moved the whole camp following the milling buffalo herd on foot as they migrated, grazed and continued to eat. Domestic dogs were used to pull travois (sledge of two poles) fastened with a harness. Walking Shoshoni located

Buffalo Grazing
Photo Courtesy of Nampa.net

roving bison herds in the wild for the hunt. Crawling among the buffalo concealed under a buffalo robe or a wolf skin, a hunter shot the buffalo with his bow and arrow.

Women preheated stones in a red hot fire, which were transferred into a pitch-sealed basket of water. As it came to a boil, buffalo meat was added to cook. Meat was broiled over spits. Three flat rocks (fire-dogs) supported a cooking pot over their campfires.

The Boise River Shoshoni band moved from place to place gathering food in four seasonal cycles. Combining the word for the food eaten at the time, buffalo, *(kutsen)* with the word, eater *(deka'a)* or buffalo eaters *(kutsundeka)* was how the Shoshoni designated different bands. The root eaters were the *Yambadeka'a*.

To become a man before warfare a brave learned to count coup. A coup stick was a sapling about 3-4 feet long soaked in water and bent into a curved crook decorated with feathers and paint.

Coup was counted with the touch of the hand, bow or quirt. The brave ran or rode at a gallop toward his opponent and struck him with his coup stick, then departed, showing bravery by getting in his enemies' face. Actual combat could mean loss of life.

Scalping was learned from the French; a French scalp was the size of a silver dollar; a full scalp took all of the enemy's hair and scalp. The quantity of scalps showed bravery and spread throughout other tribes. The Nez Perce were more civilized and refused to scalp. Shoshoni Indians formed extended family bands. They had political ties through kinship and dwelled in small camps. Two or three family generations dwelled in one band without a headman. Several family bands in a winter village may have had a headman or band chief, social director of ceremonies, dances, festivals.

The word chief was introduced by the white men. Indians had no terminology for chief, but they had a headman, who acted as the hunt or war leader. A war chief led his warriors in battle. A sub-chief served under the war chief. It was more or less a vote by the tribal council or sometimes the whole band to put the chief in power. A chief was usually chosen for his bravery.

The Shoshoni council members were voted in and made the important decisions for the band or tribe. The chief or head man presided. Treaties with the Indians were held in the council setting.

One deer fed a small band for 10 days. Deerskin was made into dresses, loin cloths and fine, soft moccasins. Sinew bound arrowheads to shafts and was also used in sewing.

Large herds of elk were hunted. Elk meat was an excellent staple for the Indians. The elk skin tanned hide was soft and made warm clothing and the leather moccasins were softer and suppler than buffalo leather. Elk skin dresses were popular. Sinew was used for bowstrings and arrow bindings. Bones and racks made weapons.

Squaws stripped sagebrush bark fibers and wove a type of cloth. The material was used to make a sagebrush dress or crude sandal. Rope was also fashioned from sagebrush bark. A tea was made by boiling the sagebrush berries and sagebrush was used for kindling.

Bear meat was a fine staple and fed the band for days. Food was shared communally. The fur made nice rugs or winter coats. They used the bones for tools. Claws were made into necklaces.

Appaloosa Horse, Favorite of the Nez Perce
(Courtesy of Jumper Horse/Sport)

"Spanish Mustang"
Photo courtesy www.aaanativearts.com

In the 16th century Spanish explorers brought the first modern horses from Spain aboard galleons to the Americas. Ute Indians stole horses from the Spanish and were the first American Indians to own horses.

Cortez imprisoned them for theft and forced them to work in gold mines. Ute Indians joined the Spanish in the slave trade for horses. Ute war parties rode into Shoshoni camps and captured women and children for slaves and traded them to the Spanish.

Comanche Indians were fierce Southern Plains Shoshoni, who had migrated south leaving present day Wind River, Wyoming around 1500 A.D. They continued south into present day northern Texas, to dwell and eventually expanded into New Mexico Territory.

Apaches raided the Spanish colonists in the late 1600's and stole horses from them. The Comanche, in present day Texas and New Mexico went on the warpath on moonlit nights; they slipped in and stole horses from the Apache for bravery and counted coup and raided Spanish settlements for horses.

The Comanche loved their horses and sang songs to them. They bred, trained, groomed them, tied ribbons in their manes, braided their tails and painted their horses for war. If a warrior died, his horses were killed and buried with him to ride in the afterlife.

Horses strayed from Spanish haciendas and became feral horses that roamed the desert in numbers in a wild bunch. Mares were stolen by wild stallions. Thousands of wild mustangs have roamed free for hundreds of years in the American southwest. A frightened herd of mustangs exploding into a stampede is a marvelous sight to behold.

Hee-Bee-Tee-Tse, Shoshoni, in his headdress, trade beads, & fur wrapped braids.
(Photo Courtesy of Azusa Publishing, L.L.C.)

Comanche Indians became experienced riders and could ride up on a feral horse and encircle its head with a lasso in the wild. They became excellent horse handlers and breeders, also. The Comanche Indian horsemen captured wild horses best in the cold of winter, when they were undernourished, more gaunt, starving and weak. When the Comanche horsemen caught a mare with foal, the mother slowed and stayed with her colt and two horses were caught.

Mustangs were stolen from ranchos in northern Mexico and Texas. They thought horses were there for the taking. The Comanche amassed thousands of horses. Wealth in horses came in the number of head owned. A chief might have collected 1,000 ponies.

Horses revolutionized the Indian life way changing their warfare, hunting, camp and seasonal moves. Comanche horsemen also caught Cayuses on a hot summer day. A wild bunch would graze on dry grasses and develop a thirst. Hot and sweaty, the wild mustangs galloped to the nearest water hole to drink until their bellies were full of water. When the horses attempted to run, being fat and sluggish, they were easy to catch.

One method of catching horses, used by the Kiowa and Comanche was the corral method. The corral was built near a watering hole. The wild horses were driven into a v-shaped enclosure. When they were in the corral, the gate was then closed. Some corrals were built large enough to hold several hundred horses and used part of its natural surroundings for the enclosure.

The Indian technique of breaking horses was effective. Several Indians held the horse, using lassoes; the feral horse was jerked off its feet, hardly breathing. As the noose was tightened, it

24

restricted the horse's air supply. It lay on the ground gasping for air; the warrior then relaxed the lasso. The lathered horse arose, weak and trembling, while the "Horse Whisperer" stroked its ears, forehead and nose. The mustang's captor then blew into its nostrils. Next, the brave bridled the horse, mounted it and rode away. The Comanche Indians had a way with horses. Pack horses were broken in to haul loads using rocks to represent weight they would be carrying.

Indian saddles the horsemen used were of two general types: the pad saddle and the frame saddle. The pad saddle was popular with the Comanche Indians. It was made from two pieces of leather sewn together and stuffed with either feathers or grass.

The frame saddle of bison bone, wood or deer antler was light weight. Wet rawhide was stretched over it and shrunk to size. The saddle weighed three pounds. The woman's saddle was of this type.

Although the Comanche had horses later, they became the most expert horsemen and the fiercest warriors of any tribe of Indians of the Plains. The Comanche chased Ute horsemen, who were hunting buffalo on the Plains, and scared them off and scattered their camps.

One scenario is that in 1700, a band of Comanche horsemen rounded up a huge herd of ponies numbering in the thousands and started on the long drive north to reach their Shoshoni counterparts.

In the 1700's, the Comanche drove horses up to Fort Hall to their Shoshoni cousins. The Comanche riders trailed the huge herd from the Southern Plains along the Rockies west across early Wyoming to trade horses to their Shoshoni brothers at Wind River. The huge herd of horses must have been a marvelous sight.

They pushed on in order to reach the Fort Hall and Boise River Shoshoni with horses. Horses grazed the plush green grasses of the Boise River bottoms, on the western boundary of Idaho Territory. It is believed that these Shoshoni were the first to receive horses in the Northwest. The Shoshoni word for horse was *kobai*. The Boise and Eastern Shoshoni Indians obtained horses about the same time as the Fort Hall Shoshoni. Northern Shoshoni Indians had horses early and became horse Indians. The Shoshoni with horses were revered over the walking Shoshoni bands.

Comanche Indians are known to have provided the northwestern Indians with horses. Another theory is that the Indians received horses early, directly from the Spanish. Others received horses from Canadian fur traders. Shoshoni Indians may have gotten horses from the Ute Indians in Colorado country. Horses transformed the Plains Indians' lives. Walking Indians became horse-mounted.

The Nez Perce received the Appaloosa horse indirectly from Comanche Indians. They bred and raised Appaloosa and other breeds of horses until their herds numbered in the thousands; it was not unusual to see the Nez Perce Indians trailing three hundred ponies.

In 1700 A.D., the horse brought change to the American Indian and revolutionized the Plains Indians life-way. The war horse provided change in warfare. The Horse and Indian Era allowed the American Indian freedom to travel great distances on the war trail.

The horse transformed the Shoshoni's way of hunting and subsistence making it easier to hunt. It gave them mobility to follow the buffalo and change seasonal cycles. A hunt chief was chosen to direct the buffalo hunt.

Shoshonis dwelled near creeks, lakes, rivers or hot springs wherever water was accessible for bathing, cooking and drinking. The women filled water pots or skins and toted them back to camp, daily. A male leaving camp carried a water-filled skin. Besides hauling water, the women also carried firewood back to camp. Indians found temporary refuge, taking advantage of natural caves, lava tubes, overhangs and rock shelters for refuge.

Paiutes and Shoshonis constructed pit houses that were built half above and half below ground, insulated from the heat and cold. Wooden poles were covered with earth and a roof of thatched rye grass. A hearth was used for heat and cooking.

The teepee was adapted from the Great Plains Indians. The teepee was a tent constructed over numerous lodge poles in a conical shaped framework, tied near the top, covered with buffalo skins, with a mat or hide flooring, anchored with several rocks. Skins were sewn together with sinew for teepee coverings. A tipi, teepee or wigwam was collapsible for travel; poles were drug behind a horse as a travois. The Snakes built communal sweat lodges, used by the men to socialize. Sweat baths were followed by a cold plunge. The Shoshoni walled up a running hot springs with stones making a permanent bath.

A ceremony was held when an Shoshoni Indian girl came of age, began to menstruate, and spent her menses in a hut (menstrual hut), isolated on the village perimeter. She bathed in spiritual cleansing, sprinkling juniper needles, sage, or sweet grass on the fire coals and drew smoke toward her, breathing it in.

The fur trapper named David Thompson recorded in 1730, that a battle was fought between horse-mounted Shoshoni Indians and

Hunting Buffalo Bareback
Sketch was done by Boise Artist, Len Sodenkamp.

Blackfeet Indians on foot. The Archeologist, Clark Wissler stated that both the Blackfeet and the Shoshoni Indians had horses in 1750.

In the spring, the women dug the roots of the blue camas flowers and ground them into flour in stone mortars. They then baked the flour into camas bread. The Camas Prairie was a popular place for the Bannock and Shoshoni to rendezvous and dig the camas roots. They fished the Boise River that teemed with native fish as salmon swam upstream to spawn in the spring. The Boise Shoshoni caught Chinook salmon, bull, cutthroat, rainbow, and steelhead trout, sturgeon and mountain white fish.

In summer, they fished until the salmon fishing slowed in autumn. Boise Shoshoni had a salmon fishery at the mouth of the Boise River yearly with plenty of Chinook salmon. As the salmon run ended many salmon were smoked on drying racks or stacked up to five feet high and sun dried and stored in cache pits for winter.

The Indian women made salmon pemmican. Pemmican was a delicacy of smoked dried strips of salmon and berries, especially chokecherries and fat ground in mortars, pressed into cakes, saved in salmon skins or woven sagebrush fiber bags and stored underground in caches for winter. Pemmican was made from bison meat, ground in a buffalo skin mortar with berries and fat and made into cakes. Salmon swam up river to spawn in the Boise River until 1860, when the phenomena ended.

Ryegrass was roasted and ground into flour. Sunflower seeds were sun-dried and shelled for gravy. Buffalo, roots, salmon and wild vegetables were staples. Beaters separated seeds from the husks collected in winnowing trays the chaff separated, heated and dried.

29

50 In the autumn, berries, nuts and seeds were gathered. Seeds were separated from the husks with beaters and collected into winnowing trays to separate out the chaff, heated and dried for storage in caches. Foodstuffs were pre-cooked, prepared and placed in an underground cache, a pit in the ground about three feet square and one foot deep, covered with pine boughs for storage.

Salmon season ended and the Boise Shoshoni hosted their annual Salmon Fest where the Boise River flowed into the Snake River until late autumn. The terrain was level with rich grasses, shade from cottonwood trees, cool water and plenty of salmon.

The festivities carried over into the Trade Fair extravaganza. The valley was called "Peace Valley," a special meeting place for celebrating, dancing, festivals, fishing, gambling, horse racing, merry making, playing games, romance and trading. They traded arrow heads, bows, horses, knives, lodge-poles, pelts, wives and other items.

After the Comanche brought the horse, horse complexes sprang up across the Northwest. The Mandan, Cheyenne and Eastern Shoshoni had trade centers, too. The Comanche traded horses to the east to tribes like the Ponca and Otoe Indians. By driving thousands of horses up north, the Comanche nearly single-handedly populated the Pacific Northwest with horses.

Buffalo in the Shoshoni language was "k'utsun." The Shoshoni were classified as "Plains Indians" because they had hunted the buffalo on horseback. " Madsen referred to a band of Bannock hunters that trekked to the Upper Missouri as a "tribal unit."

In late summer, the Kutsundeka crossed to the Upper Missouri to hunt buffalo in present day Montana, carefully crossing

Beaver dam built from gnawed trees partially
submersed under water.
(Photo Courtesy of Ned Eddins)

American Beaver
(Photo Courtesy of Wikimedia)

enemy lands invading Blackfeet and Crow Indian country. Shoshoni rode cautiously on horseback passing along single file and undetected through enemy territory, where enemy bands might attack just to take horses.

For their own preservation, these Snake River tribes, like the Plateau bands formed militant hunting parties in large numbers of socio-political allies to hunt bison. Parties of Bannock, Shoshonis, Flathead, and Nez Perce Indians rode in numbers to the Upper Missouri River Country trekking for miles to follow the buffalo onto the Plains. They had a fighting chance of hunting the needed buffalo and not losing their scalps. Scouts advanced to locate the herd.

Riding at a gallop alongside the thundering herd, a hunter singled out a choice bison; he spurred his pony alongside, shot an arrow between its ribs, penetrated a lung, and dropped the beast.

Another scenario, a hunter might ride alongside the buffalo and bring it down with a few quick jabs of his lance. They could kill enough buffalo to feed their families for some time.

Meat was dried, jerked, and packed on mules. Hunters led pack mules laden with jerky and robes back to their encampment. Jerky was cached for the long winter. Buffalo skins made warm robes.

Women cooked the meat on spits over the fire for a feast. A hunter shot enough buffalo to feed the family. Buffalo was at the top of the food chain. The buffalo was the life blood the Plains Indians.

After the hunt the warriors skinned the buffalo. Hides were stretched out by driving pegs into the ground around the perimeter and the women used hide-scrapers to remove the flesh from the hides.

The Buffalo Utility

Buffalo- clan symbol, totem
Bladder- medicine bags, quill & sinew pouches
Bones- game dice, awls, burins & needles
Brains- to cure hides, robes
Buckskin- moccasins, shirts, pouches, quivers
Buffalo chip- fuel for fires, signals
Ears- ornamentation
Entrails- heart & liver eaten
Flesh- meat, jerky, pemmican, & ribs
Fur- blankets, robes
Hair- braided rope, bridals halters
Hides- teepee covering, robes, moccasins
Hind leg- pre-shaped moccasins & boots
Hooves- glue, rattles
Horns- cups, ladles, spoons
Meat- food, jerky, pemmican
Muscle- bows, thread, sinew
Rawhide- clothing, drums, saddles, stirrups
Scalp and horns- headdress, Sun Dance
Scrotum- rattles
Shoulder blade- hoe
Skin- clothing, moccasins, teepees
Sinew- arrows, sewing, binding
Skull- Sun Dance, sacred, prayer
Stomach- buckets, cooking vessel
Tail- whips, medicine switch, fly brush
Teeth- necklaces, ornaments
Tongue- good meat

Brains were removed from the skulls and the solution rubbed into the skins. Skins were processed in warm water and hung from a tree branch about shoulder level. Hides were again scraped to give them flexibility. The hump was removed and the skin stitched.

John Coulter and George Droulliard were fur trapping legends by the time that they joined the Manuel Lisa party with the St. Louis Missouri Fur Trade Company, around 1809. At the Three Forks of the Missouri in the spring of 1810 they assisted in building "Henry's Fort" on Henry's Fork, on the north fork of the Snake River.

French trappers named "Riviera Bois" or Boise River. "Bois" means wooded area in French, the source of the name, Boise City, Idaho. The Boise River was used by Shoshoni and French for years.

In 1819, Donald McKenzie, a peacemaker, attempted to raise a fur fort in Bannock country and held talks among the tribes on the Little Lost River with the Bannock and Shoshoni Indians.

Mackenzie met with Chief Peiem (Big Jim) and Chief Amaketsa in 1820. He initiated peace negotiations and had permission to trap in Indian country and reached Indians on snowshoes. The Indians remained peaceful because of Mackenzie's negotiations

He crossed over the Blues with a large brigade and left six Iroquois Indians at the second Fort Boise with food, gear and traps. He took a brigade in boats, up the Snake River and dropped off the trappers at outposts, reaching the Bear River. On Mackenzie's return to "Fort Boise," the Iroquois had scattered to various nearby villages. The Shoshoni traded furs to the Nez Perce, who took them to the British fur forts on the Columbia.

Fort Snake (Boise) Drawing- In 1834, the Hudson's Bay Company traded with the Western Shoshoni and Northern Paiute Indians. The Whitman party arrived at Fort Boise in 1836.

(Artist's conception by Boise artist Len Sodenkamp)

The Hudson's Bay Company rivaled other fur companies on the Snake River. Employees, Ogden, Ross and Work trapped the Snake River Plain early. A famous early trader, Peter Skene Ogden recorded the first written Shoshoni history.

In 1819, Spain ceded her right to Idaho Territory. Russia ceded her rights to the Pacific Northwest in 1824.

John McLaughlin founded Fort Vancouver and built the fort in 1825 on the north bank of the Columbia, the hub of trade in the western hemisphere, as headquarters for the Hudson's Bay Company in northwest America. McLaughlin had over 34 outposts, 24 ports, six ships, and 600 employees, including Hawaiians, Chelas, Cree, Irish, Iroquois and Scot peoples. Included was a dairy, distillery, fields, fruit orchards, a garden, sawmill, ship yard and tannery.

John McKay worked 5 years as clerk at Fort Astoria. Northwest Company bought the Astor Company. Hudson's Bay Company chose the uncharted region that became Idaho as the site for their fort. McLaughlin selected McKay to build it. He chose the Reed and Mackenzie's site on Idaho Territory's western border.

Shoshoni Indians, who had held their Salmon fishery at the mouth of the Boise River for years, warned McKay not to build the fort there; that the river would "change its mind." This prophecy would come to haunt him.

In 1834, Thomas McKay built "Fort Snake." of cottonwood to serve as a fur fort for the Hudson's Bay Company who bankrolled McKay and hired him as a factor, in the position of clerk. Fort Snake (Fort Boise) was completed for the Hudson's Bay Company and served as both a general store and trading post. A ferry crossing and

36

stage stop were added later. The fort was a stockade, with cool water, hot spring, garden, horse pasture, a green grassy valley, with cottonwood trees and a circle of Indian teepees.

In 1834, the Hudson's Bay Company acquired Fort Snake and Fort Hall along the Snake River to trade furs with the local Indians. Fort Snake became an important stop along the Oregon Trail for emigrants fording the Snake there. Indians and mountain men came to trade with their furs; wagon trains stopped there, too.

A fact that most Idahoans don't know is that from 1834-1856 the British flag flew over both Fort Snake (Fort Boise) and Fort Hall. Western Shoshoni and Northern Paiute Indians brought furs to the forts in trade for bright colored beads and commodities. Hudson's Bay trappers hunted beaver in brigades and brought furs to Fort Snake, as did free trappers.

McKay was appointed chief trader and led trappers on the Snake River Plain. Mountain men often took Indian women for brides, forming a bond. They lived off of the land like the Indian. Jim Bridger and Kit Carson were independent traders, who both married Indian brides. John Freemont and his guide, Kit Carson led expedition parties on the Oregon Trail.

Freemont wrote a guide that served as a map for immigrants to Oregon and also for gold miners. In 1842, Freemont observed the village of Shoshoni Chief Amaroko with over 75 lodges and a large herd of horses on the Boise River.

During the gold rush of 1862 thousands of miners overran Indian lands in the Boise Basin and on the Salmon River. The Shoshoni had to move the Salmon Festival north to "Weiser country.

"Ground Hog"
(Photo Courtesy of Wikimedia.org)

CHAPTER TWO
THE BRUNEAU RIVER SHOSHONI

Shoshoni bands called the Bruneau River Shoshoni the Groundhog-eaters or *"Yahan-deka"* in their tongue. They hunted the groundhog (yaha) or rock-chuck that lived in the high rocky ridges. In early spring, communal drives were used for the sage hen (called fool hens) another name for a prairie chicken or sage grouse. During mating season, the male sage-hen *(hutsa)* performed a mating dance strutting in front of the hens. Roosters made off-and-on popping sounds by puffing up and releasing air-sacks on their necks.

The Shoshoni community surrounded the hens in a huge circle, beat the ground with clubs and gave off war whoops, closing in on them. They flew and then landed a short distance ahead. Sage-hen never flew far enough to escape, but were entangled in net snares and they captured the grouse for a feast. Another way was the magic of a Shoshoni shaman, disguised as an antelope (under an antelope skin). He stalked the sage hen, crawled on all fours and drove them into the netting the Indians had placed over the sagebrush.

In the spring they went up into the foothills onto the Camas Prairie to harvest the blue camas lily. Camissia Quamash was the camas with the edible blue flower. The women dug camas roots; they were piled in small mounds and sun-dried. The tuber, the shape of an onion, had a black outer husk layer that was removed. The bulb was ground in stone mortars into flour and was then baked into camas bread. Another camas variety with a white flower was very poisonous and was not to be eaten; it was called the death camas plant.

The people lodged on the Bruneau River drainage and depended on berries, fish, groundhog, grouse, rabbit, roots, sage hen, and seeds. Fleshy fruits and seeds were consumed including false dandelion, service berry, bear-berry, big sagebrush and Oregon grape. Pig weed, miner's lettuce, shooting star, fireweed, prickly pear cactus were all edible and eaten. The American bistort, bitterroot, camas and cattail were also edible native plants common to the Idaho Great Basin dug for the food value.

Women dug cat-tail, sego and water cress bulbs. Wild carrots and young cattail bulbs were eaten raw. Potherbs were harvested adding salad greens to their diet.

In the summer they fished until salmon season slowed in the fall and caught mountain whitefish, bull trout and rainbow trout in the Bruneau River. The Shoshoni were called salmon-eaters (*Agaideka*).

Groundhogs (*yaha*) or ground squirrels (*sippe*) were caught in late spring, while they were fat from winter hibernation. Small animals were caught in snares or deadfalls. This trap employed a heavy weight when the trap was triggered that fell on the prey. Groundhogs (marmots) were hunted and caught in their lair. The hunter baited a sharp hardwood hook on a line and dropped it down into the burrow and pulled up when the groundhog took the bait.

The groundhog was gutted and prepared by making a slit inside of the front leg. The other front leg was then inserted into the slit. The meat was skewered with a sharp stick. The skin was left intact and the hair singed off in a pit fire, covered with hot coals and left to roast. With the skin peeled off, the meat was eaten; it was delicious. Sometimes they stewed the meat.

Jack rabbits multiplied at a rapid rate causing a population explosion and rabbits everywhere. The Bruneau Shoshoni held rabbit drives in autumn, when the rabbits' fur was the thickest, but they were hunted all year. The whole community participated. The rabbit chief (*kammu taikwahni*) directed the event. Forming a huge circle the Shoshonis beat the bushes with sticks and drove rabbits into the center nets. Ensnared, they were slaughtered, skinned and dressed. The pelts were cut into strips and rolled up and sewn into rabbit fur blankets. Two hundred rabbit fur strips made one blanket.

The Bruneau Shoshoni erected shanties in the hot desert, called brush huts and found food in the desert. A shade house was ideal in hot weather constructed of willows, covered with fresh, green, sweet smelling birch leaf branches for the roof. It provided cool shade. The brush huts served as storage for baskets, cooking pots, digging sticks, mortars, water jugs, and winnowing baskets that were all stored there.

During Indian summer pine nuts were harvested. The pine nut eaters were the "*tubadeka*." The Indians danced for three nights. As the dance ended, the people bathed to cleanse themselves and the shaman said a prayer to the four winds and the Great Spirit for a good harvest. Pine nuts were good fresh and roasted or stored in the ground under pine boughs for the winter or ground in mortars. Pine nuts ground into flour was mixed with water to make an excellent gravy. Autumn ended; they returned to their winter haunt and the next cycle.

Insects were collected using drives communally. Crickets and grasshoppers were caught in nets and ground in mortar and pestles into paste that were roasted on a stick or stored and made into cakes for their winter consumption. The paste was about 97% protein.

41

As autumn (*Yepani*) began, berries, nuts and seeds were gathered. In the early fall wild rye-grass seeds had ripened. The seeds were picked and separated from the husks with beaters, collected into winnowing trays and were thrown into the air to separate out the chaff in the wind. Seeds were heated and dried for storage in cache pits or ground into flour before it was made into an Indian rye-bread.

In the autumn, many edible berries were harvested. Buck berries, choke-cherries, currants, and service berries were ground into a pulp, sun-dried, and made into a delicious pudding.

As sunflowers withered, the seeds became exposed. The Newe (Shoshoni) women gathered them for storage in baskets underground covered with green branches. They ground sunflower seeds in mortar and pestles into flour used as gravy. Currants and buck berries were eaten off the vine, dried for winter or ground into pudding. As autumn ended, the band returned to their winter haunt.

In winter, (*Tommo*) in the Shoshoni dialect cycle, wind sheltered stream valleys were chosen and protected from the frigid wind. Fish were caught through the ice. Beaver, deer, ground hog, grouse, quail, rabbit, and sage hen were also hunted for sustenance.

The Boise River and Bruneau River Shoshonis bonded and intermarried. The Bruneau River band was not horse mounted until they became intermixed with the Boise River Shoshoni.

Some tribes practiced the use of scaffold and tree burials, but the Shoshoni preferred subterranean burials, instead. The deceased's body was adorned in his best war garments and sprinkled with sacred red ochre. The corpse was wrapped in a buffalo skin and further wrapped in wet skins and sewn to be mummified. The body was transported on a horse-drug travois to the gravesite and placed in a deep crevice; his bow, arrows, lance, war shield, and medicine pouch were laid beside his body. Large rocks were piled over the body to appear natural and preventing predators from digging up the remains. Cemeteries were taboo. Any graveyard intruders were attacked.

The Treaty of Boise in 1864 was written at Fort Boise. The simple document said that the Shoshoni Indians gave up the Boise River drainage for care under the U.S. Government and were treated as a favored tribe; however the treaty took away the Indians lifeblood. It was never legally ratified. At a later date, Governor Caleb Lyon wrote another treaty with the Bruneau Shoshoni.

A special agent was assigned to the Boise and Bruneau Shoshoni Indians in 1867 and 200 Indians in the Boise City vicinity waited in a camp for assignment. About 850 Bruneau Shoshonis and 150 Bannocks wintered above Boise City. They were moved further north to hunt and fish; 1,000 Snakes camped above Boise City. They asked for provisions and blankets for winter. Due to severe winters and lack of food, Indians were dying of exposure and starvation.

Territorial Governor Ballard ordered Agent Powell to move the Bruneau River and Boise River Shoshoni to Fort Hall Indian Reservation on March 13, 1869. The Bannock Indians had first been moved to Fort Hall Indian Reservation, named for the fur Fort Hall.

A special Indian Agent moved the Western Shoshoni, the Boise River and Bruneau River Shoshoni to Fort Hall Reservation for their own safety. The reservation was about 1,800,000 acres and lay along the Snake River at the junction of the Portneuf River.

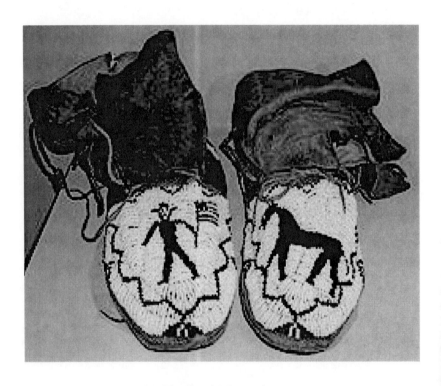

Shoshoni Moccasins
(Photo Courtesy of Wikimedia.org)

CHAPTER THREE
WEISER RIVER SHOSHONI

The Weiser Shoshoni lodged in the Weiser River Valley in the rugged mountains of west-central Idaho Territory and occupied the high valleys of the Upper Weiser River and the Lower Hell's Canyon, east to the middle fork of Salmon Country. They evolved from a mountain band of Sheep-eater Indians, who had moved up into the mountains to escape aggression from fierce tribes like the Blackfoot and Sioux Indians. In the same way, the Weiser Indians withdrew to the secluded mountain passes of Indian Valley, Payette and the Weiser River Valleys to lodge in their own solitude.

The Shoshonis on the western tributaries of the Snake were called "*Seewooki*," in their dialect. Weiser Indians were Uto-Aztecan speakers. It was a slow sing-song dialect marked with regular rhythm and rhyme and their language was like other Northern Shoshonis. *Tegwani* were talkers, who spoke in council of the location of the buffalo herds or food gathering areas for the local rounds and sometimes they talked for a long time.

Weiser Indians were extended family bands of Shoshoni. The Weiser group was a mixed band of Bannock, Mountain Shoshoni and Nez Perce Indian nomads. They referred to themselves as "the people" the *newe* or *numunuh* and coexisted peacefully with most Nez Perce and Paiutes. Nomadic Cayuse, Flathead, and Spokane Indians roamed western Idaho Territory to fish, hunt and trade.

The Weiser Shoshoni traded for horses shortly after 1700 A.D. and became horse mounted. A pony served as a mount to hunt that could traverse the mountain passes. The horse was invaluable.

45

Shoshoni were grass-weavers known as the "grass house people." The Weiser River band lodged in wickiup shelters, which were conical shaped dwellings on the order of a tipi. Willow uprights were tied at the top, thatched with brush or sewn woven grass mats. Villages consisted of 15 to 20 lodges that housed 75 to 100 people.

Weiser women made excellent basketry and pottery of local materials. Basket bowls, fish baskets, seed baskets, water jugs and winnowing baskets were crafted of reeds and grasses. The pottery was crafted from clay from the river bottoms and baked.

As the Salmon Festival ended, the annual trade fair began. Weiser Indians conducted trade on their lands with the Boise River Shoshoni hosting neighboring Indian tribes at the confluence of the Boise, Malheur, Owyhee, Payette and Weiser Rivers with the Snake River on a large island near Payette, Idaho. The fair had been pushed north after the paleface intervention.

The Bannock, Flathead, Nez Perce, and Eastern Shoshoni were some of the tribes that met to gamble, barter and trade. Bannocks brought buffalo robes to trade for horses and bartered for salmon. Women were traded for wives. The Indians traded arrow heads, arrows, bows, horses, knives, pelts, and other items.

Arapahoe and Cheyenne braves drug cedar lodge poles behind their horses for trade. Northern Paiutes produced flaked obsidian arrowheads. Umatilla and Cayuse Indians traveled inland with ornamental seashells from the Pacific Ocean to barter and trade. Peaceable Indians were welcomed to come and trade their wares. Many Nez Perce lodges (a unit of measure), were there to swap horses. They brought beautiful Appaloosa horses and other breeds.

Weiser Indians hunted antelope and buffalo in the valleys, fished the flowing streams and moved on the land hunting and gathering along the pristine river valleys. The Weiser coalesced with other Shoshoni to cross the Bannock Trail to the Upper Missouri for the annual buffalo hunt. Then they were referred to as the *Kutsundeka.* If they hunted wild mountain sheep in Hells Canyon, they were called Sheep-eaters or *Tukedekas.*

Salmon was their diet at the top of the food chain. They fished for mountain white fish, rainbow or bull trout, and salmon. Their kinsmen identified them as *"Agaideka."* or the salmon-eaters, the food they ate at the time. The Weiser dwelled in Indian Valley.

The Weiser Shoshonis took salmon from the Boise, Malheur, Owyhee, Payette, and Weiser Rivers in the spring. The Weiser River and its tributaries were spawning grounds for salmon, steelhead (salmon trout), and Chinook (dog salmon), that ran the Weiser River. Salmon was smoked and baled in stacks for winter consumption. Pemmican was made with fish and berries and cached for winter.

Weiser fishermen used two parallel stone weirs (barriers) in the river about 30 yards apart to entrap sockeye (red salmon) during their runs to spawn. Weirs slowed and trapped the migrating salmon. They caught fish by hand, hooks, using nets, poison, harpoons, spears and bow and arrows. They fished on the Payette and Weiser Rivers to Payette Lake and on the south fork of the Salmon.

They killed antelope on the prairie. When deer came to the river to drink it was easy for the Shoshoni to shoot them with their bow and arrows. They shot elk, mule deer and white tail deer for subsistence. The Shoshoni trapped beaver, mink, otter and various fur

47

bearing animals for their meat and skins. Braves killed cotton tail, jack rabbit and snow-shoe rabbits with their bows.

In the spring they gathered berries, nuts, roots and seeds and gathered the balsam root, biscuit root, bitterbrush, huckleberry, lupine, pine grass, service-berry and snowberry. The Weiser Indians began their fishing season in the spring and fished until mid-autumn.

In autumn, they moved up into the mountains and gathered plants and hunted larger game. The blue flower camas root was found in the wetlands and the higher elevations from Smith's Ferry north through Long Valley into the Salmon Meadows. Women dug the camas root, their source of flour ground in mortar and pestles into meal before it was made into dough and baked it into camas bread.

In the fall they moved back down to the lower elevations and continued to fish for salmon. The fish that they caught provided food for the winter. Plump deer, fat from grazing all summer were hunted in autumn for the venison. Excellent clothiers and furriers, Weiser Indian women made tailor-fit deerskin clothing for the whole family.

In the winter, they returned to the same protected river valleys, where they could fish and hunt and the seasonal round continued.

Lewis and Clark tried unsuccessfully to find a route along the Salmon River through Weiser country. The Payette River was named for Captain Francois Payette and the Weiser River for Peter Weiser; Weiser had been a member of the Lewis & Clark Expedition.

The Peter Weiser party explored the Hell's Canyon to fish for salmon and saw an abundance of bighorn sheep and deer. Settlers called the Snakes along the Weiser River the "Weiser Shoshoni."

48

Meriwether Lewis and William Clark
Wikimedia.org

Prehistoric dog remains with human burials were discovered by Archeologists near Weiser, Idaho, where canine remains were found that radio carbon dated back to 6590 B.P. Southern Shoshoni Comanche shot and buried a number of horses for their masters' afterlife. Was this same practice performed with their dogs?

Donald Mackenzie's party crossed Weiser country along an old Indian trail later known as the "Old Boise Trail" to the Clearwater River. He was the first white man to transverse the Weiser country.

Wilson Price Hunt led the Astoria party across the Weiser in 1811 and found passage to the Hell's Canyon Gorge blocked. Returning, they saw twelve lodges on the Weiser; friendly Shoshoni shared two horses, a dog, some roots, dried cherries and fish.

Hunt attempted to get an Indian guide to lead them over the mountains. They wanted the party to stay the winter, but Hunt wanted to keep moving. The Shoshone swore the snow was waist deep and knew they would freeze. Hunt said they spoke with a forked tongue and called them women. A Shoshoni man agreed to act as their guide. The guide led them to the Snake River, to the Umatilla and the Columbia Rivers; they reached their destination at Fort Astoria. Hunt spoke of the region and the John Reid party came to the Boise area.

Lt. Bonneville was on leave from the U.S. Army and came to the Weiser region in 1832 and noted how the Shoshonis made their seasonal rounds. He met some Weiser Indians that had just traded with the Nez Perce at the mouth of the Weiser River and took note of their fine horses and good equipment. The Weisers warned him of a nearby Bannock war party. Lt. Bonneville continued into Oregon Country. Canadian traders began trapping on the Weiser River.

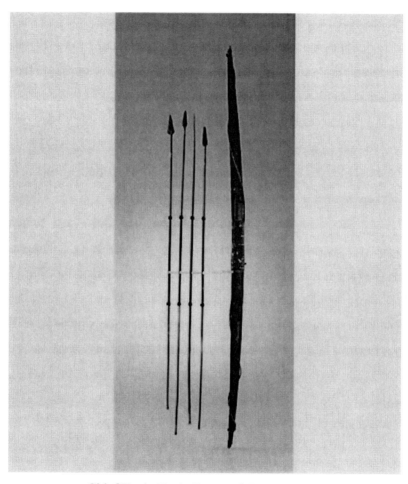

Chief Eagle Eye's Bow and Arrows
Photo Courtesy of Heritage Auction, www.HA.com

Little is known about the early life of Chief Eagle Eye except that he came from a family of Mountain Snakes and that his homeland was in the Timber Butte region. Eagle Eye grew into manhood and became a strong warrior. The Weiser's were peacemakers, a trait passed down from their ancestors.

Eagle-Eye became the last non-reservation chief of the Northern Shoshoni. His Weiser band had Sheep-eater roots, yet they lodged in the Weiser River Valley and seldom warred.

Settlers and miners started to arrive in the Weiser Valley. As the white man arrived on the scene, the Weiser shadowed them from the wilderness. The Weiser band avoided conflict with the white man and kept hidden in the mountains and remote valleys.

The steamship, "Shoshone" hauled passengers and freight between Farewell Bend and Weiser to Owyhee Crossing, 100 miles away using wood for fuel. With little fuel, they beached the ship on the Snake, but the steamship was later ordered to the Columbia for duty. The ship's captain ran Hell's Canyon rapids, causing damage. It was repaired and it ran on the Columbia River for many years.

In the 1860's the U.S. Army came. A band of Indians, assumed to be Chief Eagle-Eye's Weiser Shoshoni were observed in the Seven Devils Mountains northwest of Indian Valley.

The U.S. Army staged an offensive looking for a fight and tried to protect the settlers and miners. Howard pursued Eagle-Eye during the Snake War in 1866. Eagle Eye disappeared into the mountains and avoided capture. The search was abandoned after a report of his death in 1868.

American Indian Wickiup
Photo Courtesy of the American Library of Congress

The report came in that a band of thieving Snake Indians was camped on the headwaters of the Weiser River. The Cavalry rode out to Chief Eagle Eye's encampment in 1869. Colonel James B. Sinclair, the Commander of Fort Boise, located Eagle-Eye's group and recognized him as chief of the band that was wintering on the Little Weiser River in Indian Valley and the juncture of Crane Creek.

Sinclair's troops captured the Weiser band of 41 Shoshoni men, women and children. Chief Eagle Eye presented Col. Sinclair with his bow and arrows as a peace offering. Sinclair captured 21 horses and confiscated a large quantity of dried roots and smoked salmon the Army used to survive. Col. Sinclair and Governor Ballard realized that the Weiser Indians were peaceable and freed them.

Chief Eagle Eye's bow is a virtual masterpiece. The bow and arrows are in a private collection today. On the surface of the bow is painted, "Eagle Eye, Chief of the Weiser Snakes, August 19, 1868."

The bow is 34 inches long with a 40 pound pull. The longest arrow is 26 3/4 inches in length. It is a sinew backed composite bow with a rawhide wrapped grip over bird quills. The bowstring is made of multi-strand twisted sinew. Arrows are one piece construction fully balanced and have two parallel spirit (medicine) grooves.

In 1870, Eagle-Eye refused to go on the reservation, but other Weiser Shoshoni Indians were taken to the Fort Hall Reservation. During the Nez Perce War of 1877, Chief Eagle Eye led his band to the Malheur Reservation for their safety.

Eagle-Eye and 139 Weisers arrived at the Malheur Indian Reservation in August of 1877 with Special Agent Turner, who had escorted them there. It housed Bannock, Paiute and Shoshoni Indians

Egan was born a Cayuse Indian and raised Paiute. His Indian name was Pony Blanket. Egan married Evening Star. They had two sons and a daughter. He became a lower Malheur and Owyhee River chief, who had ties to Winnemucca and lived near the Weisers.

Another local band was led by Chief Eagle-From-the-Light. In 1872, many Paiutes moved onto the Klamath Reserve after the Snake War and faced starvation under the crooked Agent Rinehart. Pony Blanket collaborated with Chief Has-No-Horse, to free the Paiutes.

Chief Eagle Eye was a respected peace-chief and a good leader of his people, who resisted the transition to the reservation, while maintaining peace with the white man. He was not warring and distanced himself and the band he led from the white intruders. He withdrew into the valleys of the mountains in order to avoid war.

Chief Eagle Eye used his head in order to survive. It is not clear whether the Chief participated in the Bannock War, but it is known that he remained around Dry Buck and Timber Butte close to Squaw Creek, an old obsidian source of the Shoshoni, near Emmett

When it became necessary Eagle Eye and his people joined the white citizens of Emmett, Idaho. They worked alongside them in the mining and timber business, but no one turned the Indians in to the Army. They labored there for years in peace. Eagle Eye was a peacemaker and a friend to the white man.

Chief Eagle Eye passed away at the end of May 1896. In 1904, the last of his Weiser band transitioned to the Fort Hall Indian Reservation.

Sheep-eater Indians in Wickiup at a Mountain Camp
on Medicine Creek in Eastern Idaho in 1877
Photo Courtesy of the Smithsonian Institute

CHAPTER FOUR
SHEEP-EATER SHOSHONI

Mountain Snakes were isolated bands of Shoshoni Indians who ranged from the Yellowstone into the Teton Range and across the Bitterroots of Montana. The Sheep-eaters dwelled over the Salmon River Mountains of the Northern Plateau north and into the Upper Snake River Country and hunted the evasive mountain sheep.

The Sheep-eater Indians dwelled in the mountain heights and lodged in the Yellowstone Rockies above 7500 feet elevation across the Idaho-Montana border near the Blackfeet, Crow, Flathead and Shoshoni tribes from Yellowstone to the Salmon River Mountains. The Blackfeet still raided the Shoshoni bands, although they had lost nearly half of their populations to the white man's diseases and war.

An example of the way Shoshoni bands recognized each other was by the seasonal cycle of the food they ate at the time combined with the word, eater. Peers called them Sheep-eaters because they ate sheep for subsistence and hunted the obscure animals on a regular basis.

Tuka in Shoshoni meant sheep and *deka* meant eater. They were called *"Tukudekas"* or Sheep-eaters in their tongue. The *Kutsundeka* hunted buffalo and were called or the Buffalo eaters; hunting elk they were the *Padehiyadeka* or the Elk eaters.

Other tribes respected them for their lifestyle. The main diet was sheep. In the winter, they utilized snowshoes. The snowshoes were usually made of wood, but there were reports that some snowshoes were crafted of sheep horn. They skinned the animals and the women then processed the hides. Their garb was tailored from animal skins and tanned in the highest quality brown, white and yellow buckskins. Antelope skins made loin cloths.

Sheep-eaters were holy men or people of the sun; sometimes they were referred to as "Sky People." The People below were earth people. Mythical beings were the "water people." The on goers that traveled through Indian country rarely got a glimpse of them. They were seldom seen, like phantoms.

Sheep-eaters were considered the most skilled Indian hunters of the elusive wild Rocky Mountain sheep in the lofty heights and had an unusual capability to hunt sheep high up among the clouds. Sheep-eaters handcrafted bows of wood and laminated horn from the mountain sheep. The excellent laminated bows were especially fine quality and traded for five to ten good ponies.

The men used special bow and arrows to hunt antelope, bear, buffalo, cougar, deer, elk, and rabbit. They killed the game and transported it back to feed the extended family band. Mountain Snakes hunted game near the timberline in the mountain passes, where bighorn sheep, mule deer, and wapiti grazed along game trails.

Arrow shafts were crafted from dogwood or mock orange. A branch was scraped of bark, heated and straightened with an arrow wrench, abraded, smoothed and polished with stone tools. Chert or obsidian arrowheads, knives and spearheads were flaked during the slow time of winter. Arrowheads were glued into grooves in shafts with pine pitch wrapped with sinew. Arrows were fletched with owl or eagle feathers and glued into slits on the ends.

Women manufactured the family's clothing. Men's war shirts and women's dresses were made from deer, elk, and mountain

Bighorn Mountain Sheep Ram
(Photo Courtesy of Ned Eddins)

Bighorn Mountain Sheep on Snowy Slope
(Photo Courtesy of Ned Eddins)

sheep skins. Rabbit-fur blankets were used on frigid nights. Sheep-eater women sewed coyote-skin ear flaps inside men's caps and made antelope skin leggings. Two antelope or wolf-skins sewn together made blankets. A strip of fox-skin made a head band. Sheep-eater women were furriers, tanners of fine quality deer, elk, panther, and sheep skins. Moccasins were handcrafted from badger skin that was durable. Elk-skin made good supple moccasins. A one piece moccasin was made from the foreleg of a deerskin. They traded these excellent furs for ammo, awls, axes, kettles, and tobacco.

Lewis and Clark contacted the Sheep-eater Shoshoni in 1805. Lemhi Chief Cameahwait had spoken to Lewis of the "Broken Moccasin Indians," referring to the Mountain Shoshoni. Possibly their moccasins were badly worn from scampering over jagged rocks.

In his journal, Lewis depicted the Mountain Snakes as poor, destitute wretches and described their fur clothing as gaudy. He said that they were flamboyant at times, boasters who told wild stories. Lewis said they were an honest fair and generous people and never beggars. Sheep-eaters traded for guns and horses from the party.

It is hinted that the wild dogs of the Mountain Snakes were domesticated wolf pups. Lewis and Clark described seeing domestic dogs that looked like wolves the Indians used to hunt elk.

Domestic dogs were beasts of burden utilized to pull travois and haul firewood. Dogs were kept as pets and watch-dogs. Puppies made a tender meal. Dog fur was woven into woolen blankets. Dogs used for hunting looked like Russian wolfhounds. The bloodhound made good trackers. Two wolfhounds working together could cut a wild sheep from a herd and drive it into a crude corral.

Sheep-eaters dwelling in the Yellowstone Mountains late in the 19th century were seen with at least 30 pack dogs. The pack dogs carried provisions, and skins. The Indians were armed with laminated bows and obsidian tipped arrowheads. Indians carried back packs and pack-dogs were commonly used. Sheep-eaters also wove backpacks from strips of sagebrush bark constructed with skin or fiber straps. Food was wrapped in skins and was carried on their backs.

W.A. Allen had an interview with a one hundred and fifteen year old Sheep-eater woman in 1913, meaning that she was born in 1798. Her Shoshoni name meant "The-Woman-Under-the-Ground."

The-Woman-Under-the-Ground told Allen that the Tukurikas were driven south, into the hills and mountains by the Blackfeet Indians, which may be why they adapted to life in the mountain heights, forced to live among the clouds. She said they hunted mountain sheep with their sheep-horn bows and used hunting dogs.

The elder woman explained that her people lived in caves and overhangs. Instead of a teepee, they built wickiups high above their enemies. She said a wickiup was a cone-shaped hut constructed of cedar pole uprights thatched with grey moss and cemented with pine pitch. Flooring was of sheep skins. Their garb was made from skins of the antelope decorated with eagle feathers, ermine and otter skins.

The ancient one said that her people sometimes descended down to the valleys, but always returned to live high among the clouds. The one of great wisdom related how her people thrived on the mountain sheep and how the wapiti would ascend to mountain passes and the hunters would shoot them with their bow and arrows. The Sheep-eaters had excellent survival skills.

Bannock Indians in Yellowstone
Photograph Courtesy of Legends of America.com

The old woman described petroglyphs on smooth rock walls below and told of her belief that the Great Spirit etched impressions on the walls in the form of lightning strikes from above and said that her people then colored them in using paint pigment. The ancient sage also described how her people used obsidian arrow points as chisels to inscribe art forms and murals, she called painted rocks.

The old one spoke of the Sheep-eaters being Sun Worshippers. She told how her people chanted songs to the Sun. The Great Spirit was pleased and gave them plenty of sheep, meat, berries to eat, good drinking water and the snows to keep the flies down.

Shoshoni mythology portrayed Sheep-eaters as "wild men, a vanishing race of pygmies. "They were described as shy, retiring, and dwarflike. Shrouded in mystery, their history and ethnology was not recorded because of their dwelling in high elevations.

In 1872, the U.S. Park Service established the Yellowstone National Park and banned the Shoshoni Indians from residing there. Sheep-eaters resisted as long as they could or were confined to reservations outside of the park, as no threat to tourists.

The Sheep-eater Indians were removed from their homeland in Yellowstone and transitioned to the Lemhi Reservation in 1875 and lived as one band with the Bannock and Shoshoni Indians.

The Sheep-eaters were pressured to join in the Bannock War of 1878. In 1879, Col. Reuben Bernard and his 1st Cavalry left the Boise Barracks and rode hard north to intercept the Sheep-eaters as the Sheep-eater War erupted. There were only two skirmishes; fifty one Sheep-eater men, women and children were captured. The war was won and the Mountain Snake Indians were confined to reserves.

Steelhead Salmon
Photo Courtesy of Wikimedia.org

Wild Trout, food source of the Lemhi Indians
(Author photo)

CHAPTER FIVE
SALMON-EATER SHOSHONI

The Northern Plateau is mountainous with forests, lakes, rivers, heavy precipitation and a climate change from the Great Basin. Trees grew above the tree line of the Rockies and along rivers. Northern Shoshoni Indians that dwelled in the Plateau region in the Lemhi Valley and Salmon River Mountains north of the Snake River Plains were the Salmon-eater and Sheep-eater Shoshonis, who were closely associated. The Salmon River drains into the Middle Fork of the Snake River.

Salmon-eater Shoshonis ranged from the Salmon River area into western Montana. Sheep-eater Shoshoni dwelled high in the Salmon River Mountains above. Salmon-eaters lodged south of the Nez Perce, who heavily influenced their culture. Salmon-eaters intermarried with Bannock, Nez Perce, Paiute, and other Shoshoni.

In the Northern Plateau, the Salmon-eater or "Agai-deka" depended on fish for sustenance. The Salmon-eaters dwelled along the Salmon River drainage; fish made up over half of their diet. Chinook salmon swam upstream to spawn. They caught bull, cutthroat and rainbow trout, Chinook salmon, mountain whitefish, steelhead, sturgeon and squawfish. Mountain lakes held land-locked kokanee salmon. With the Salmon River's four large tributaries and yearly salmon runs, the Plateau region was a Mecca for inhabitance.

Longhouse dwellings of the Lemhi Shoshoni were rectangular and partly underground. Walls were logs lashed together fastened to uprights. The roof was a woven thatch and the floor was mat. The longhouse dwellings contained hearths.

President Thomas Jefferson in 1803 authorized the military expedition of Meriwether Lewis and William Clark of the Corp of Discovery with 31 army corps and hired men to cross-country to the Pacific Ocean. Lewis and Clark were the first explorers west of the Mississippi, who opened up the Western hemisphere. The Corp journeyed from St. Louis to the upper Missouri River Valley region of North Dakota and reached Fort Mandan.

Toussaint Charbonneau, a French-Indian fur trapper, greeted them. They hired him as interpreter and met his wife, Sacajawea or "Bird Woman," in the Hidatsa language. At age 16, Sacajawea, a Lemhi Shoshoni, was captured by Hidatsa Indians. Charbonneau won Sacajawea in a gambling game with them and took her for a wife.

In 1804-1805, Lewis and Clark wintered in Fort Mandan, where Sacajawea gave birth to a son, Baptiste, who Clark called Pompey. In the spring, they canoed the Missouri through "grizzly country." Reaching the Missouri's headwaters the Corp descended the western slopes of the Rocky Mountains, low on supplies.

The party counted on reaching Sacajawea's Lemhi people for help. "Fort Colt Killed Camp" was the site in 1805, where Lewis and Clark resorted to killing a young colt to prevent starving. The party continued and Sacajawea began to recognize landmarks of her homeland. Chief Cameahwait of the Lemhi Shoshoni was quite surprised when a party of famous white men, "*Taibo*" in Shoshoni, arrived, but was more surprised when a member of the party turned out to be his sister, Sacajawea, who had been taken by the Hidatsa Indians. She rushed toward Chief Cameahwait and sucked her fingers, the Shoshoni sign of kinship.

66

Sacajawea spoke no English, only Shoshoni and Hidatsa dialects. She and Charbonneau worked as a team. Sacajawea translated a message from Shoshoni into Hidatsa, while Charbonneau translated Hidatsa into French. A French speaker in the party also spoke English and through the interpreters they could successfully translate between the Shoshoni Indians and Lewis and Clark.

Lewis and Clark sat cross-legged and traded with the Shoshonis. Clark was able to get provisions, pack horses and also, Old Toby, a Shoshoni guide to lead them to the Pacific. The Lewis and Clark Party bade farewell to the Shoshoni for the time being.

Canoes were sunk with big rocks and cached, for the return trip. Lewis and Clark were able to get badly needed horses from the Lemhi; horses were ridden from there. The Lemhi received the horse through trade in the 1700's and hunted buffalo on horseback.

Sacajawea canoed with her papoose in a cradle board, strapped to her back. Once, the boat swamped and Sacajawea saved several precious parcels. She was very ill on the trip for about a week.

In present day Idaho, Lewis and Clark also contacted the Nez Perce Indians and traded guns and ammunition for horses. They also traded beads to the Nez Perce. The journey was a tedious 8,000 mile venture over perilous rugged terrain, traveling to the Pacific Ocean and back.

The Nez Perce Indians provided a great feast with gifts for the explorers, who were given safe passage through their country. Lewis and Clark sat down on a blanket to trade with the Nez Perce Indians, who said "no want red beads, want blue beads," the pale blue donut shaped beads they had obtained from Spanish explorers.

Lewis and Clark camped in Nez Perce country and built dugout canoes at a site called "Canoe Camp." Trees were felled along the river for dugouts to be fashioned from logs as needed. They passed through the Rocky Mountains by canoeing the Clearwater River to the Snake River to the Columbia and on to the Pacific Ocean.

The Lewis and Clark party waited at Long Camp (Camp Chopunnish) in East Kamiah until spring to cross the snow-covered mountains. On the return trip from the Pacific, Sacajawea had turned out to be a huge asset to Clark and was honored for her achievements.

The great Oregon Trail and the Mormon Trail became main routes for thousands of travelers. Rumors were that white men were planning the Indians' demise; Indians began raiding wagon trains. As American settlers traveled west by wagon train Indians attacked them. In 1851, the Indians and emigrants fought skirmishes. Thirty two settlers were killed, but emigrants continued pushing westward. Indian Wars erupted and military forts were needed for protection.

In 1853 the Walkara War erupted between the Ute Indians and the Mormons in Utah Territory, but a treaty was signed. In 1855, Mormon missionaries arrived to erect Fort Lemhi among the Salmon-eaters. Chief Snag welcomed them and offered land on the river to build a mission. Brigham Young visited the mission and authorized the first marriages in the history of the Utah colony between Mormon brethren and Indian brides.

They renamed the Salmon-eaters, Lemhi Indians. "Lemhi" did not exist historically until missionaries came to the Salmon River Mountains in 1855. They called them Sacajawea's people. The name, "Lemhi" came from the book of Mormon.

They planted potatoes, sowed wheat and built houses. Grasshoppers swarmed the crops, but they sewed more. Soon 24 lodges of Nez Perce arrived at the mission and began trading horses to the Shoshoni for buffalo robes.

Mormons learned the Shoshoni dialect and Indians attended church. Chief Snag was baptized into the Mormon Church. Brigham Young advised Snag to make peace with the Bannock and Nez Perce. Young learned thousands of soldiers were en route from Washington D.C. to Salt Lake to suspend him as governor and ordered his "Sons of Dan army" back to California.

Making peace with other tribes ended the old ways of raiding for horses from the Nez Perce and fighting. In 1858, the Lemhi people resented Chief Snag's peaceful ways and in retaliation, they took Chief Snag's cattle and fish he had caught.

Incited by the Utah War of 1857, February 28, 1858, a mixed band of Snakes attacked the Lemhi Mission, killed two Mormon settlers, and drove off 250 head of cattle and 29 head of horses.

Brigham Young ordered them to vacate. They left 200 bushels of wheat for Chief Snag and 1,000 bushels of wheat for the mission.

The Utah War made Indian women fearful of reprisal. September 13, 1860, the Myers train straggled behind other wagons and was attacked by Indians resulting in the Salmon Falls Massacre.

In 1862, Agent Owen noted a number of Mountain Snakes wintered near his lodge. He routinely issued portions of beef and flour to help them endure the hard winter. They suffered from starvation; a band of those poor wretches needing food rustled cattle from a settler.

Shoshoni Indian Scout
Photo Courtesy of
Legends of America.com

CHAPTER SIX
FORT HALL SHOSHONI

The Shoshoni people near Fort Hall were called the "Sagebrush Knoll People" or "*Pohogue*" in their dialect. Fort Hall Shoshoni lodged near Fort Hall Trading Post in the river bottoms.

The Fort Hall Shoshoni hunting grounds was in the Snake River Valley, on the Camas Prairie and in the Portneuf and Sawtooth Mountains. Prehistorically, the Bannock, an offshoot of the Northern Paiute, migrated near the Fort Hall Shoshoni, bonded and intermarried with them merging as one tribe; the romance continues today.

The climate around Fort Hall was semi-arid with desert terrain. The bottom land was sagebrush-covered prairie; three rivers broke the plain: the Blackfoot, Portneuf and Snake rivers.

The Fort Hall Shoshoni spoke the Uto-Aztecan language, but had a different dialect than other Shoshonean peoples. The Uto-Aztecan language group was shared by seven bands in the Idaho region. The Eastern Shoshoni and other groups in the Great Basin shared the same language.

Before the teepee, early Shoshonis built pit houses constructed half below ground and half above ground, with insulation from the heat and cold and a hearth for warmth and cooking. Houses were of mud with wooden roof supports and thatched rye grass roofs.

The medicine man used his magic to call the buffalo herd to him. Pedestrian Indians located wild bison herds. The whole camp followed the buffalo as they migrated. The buffalo sustained the Plains Indians with millions in herds on the Great Plains.

Fort Hall Shoshoni caught Yellowstone cutthroat and rainbow trout in nearby creeks. The Snake River below the Salmon Falls teemed in wild salmon that came to spawn and there was a fishery held annually with a salmon run in the spring and one in the fall.

Near Glenn's Ferry the Snake Indians had a communal fishery. They used rocks to build dams called weirs (still seen by air today) to trap Chinook salmon and caught fish by hand, bone hooks, nets, spears or stunned them with poison. Their diet was fish.

The Snake Indians husband's extended family lived in the territory of the tribe of his father. Property passed down through the father's line. Shoshoni practiced arraigned marriages and practiced polygamy, the act of having more than one mate. A man marrying an Indian bride would also take her younger sisters for wives; all dwelt in the same lodge. Non-related wives lived in separate lodges.

Tattoos were common for the Plains Indians. The Shoshoni practiced the tattooing of both sexes. Geometric shapes and figures were popular.

The eagle was a symbol for the Indian. It meant strength in his dream quests. Eagle feathers made beautiful headdresses and costumes, worn in dances and ceremonies. Shoshoni caught young eagles and hawks and kept them in stick cages for the feathers.

The Shoshoni loved to play games. La Crosse was played with a racket and a deerskin ball. Young Shoshonis ran races. Game-pieces were made of bone or stone. A guessing game of which hand held the game-stone behind the back was played. Indian boys lagged a piece to the line drawn in the dirt. One would throw a game-piece while others tossed in an attempt to hit the piece was another game.

They played stick games. The young Indians ran foot races. The little girls, like girls worldwide, played with dolls. Musical instruments were wooden flutes, mariachis, rattles and eagle-bone whistles. Rattles were made of gourds, hooves, and turtle shell. The whole village danced.

Shoshoni did the Back and Forth Dance, Round Dance, Scalp Dance, Sun Dance and War Dance. Women danced the Scalp Dance round a scalp pole to the beat of drums and wooden rasps. The social director conducted the dance. The Indians loved music and dance.

The Cry Dance was done in mourning for a loved one who died. The Rain Dance and Warm Dance related to weather. They formed a huge circle surrounding the camp and danced all night. The all night vigil uplifted their spirits.

The Sun Dance was borrowed from other Plains tribes yet this description is similar to the ceremony of the Shoshoni. The people assembled and a tree for the center pole of the Sun Lodge was cut down and trimmed. The next day the sun pole was raised.

Two lodges were joined as one huge ceremonial Sun Lodge and the high priest or lodge builder was in charge. The Sun Lodge was a huge network of lodge poles, constructed for a large arena.

The people assembled to fast and pray. Some made vows. They chanted and gave incantations. Others sang sacred songs. There was dancing and singing, accompanied by drums, eagle bone whistles, mariachis and buffalo hide rattles for the dance. The Shoshoni danced in solemn celebration to their Sun god. In the next four days, the camp was made ready and a big feast was held. War bonnets trailed down the backs of the "Sun Chiefs," representing the buffalo's back. Warriors boasted of their feats on the war trail. Women wore brightly colored dresses and glass beads. The Sun Dance was the favorite celebration of the Fort Hall Shoshoni.

The Sun Dance was a religious ceremony for a promise to the Sun. If a warrior was spared death from the enemy, he might make a vow to the Sun-god to dance the Sun Dance. The Shoshoni made offerings to the Sun god. This practice was their religious duty. They sang offering songs to the Sun god, the supreme deity. His wife was the Moon and their son was the Morning Star.

On the day of the celebration, a sacred woman made a solemn vow to the Sun god for the recovery of the sick. The woman, who was chosen to serve as medicine woman for the Sun Dance had to be true to her husband and had led a virtuous life to qualify to assume the role of making the solemn vow. The rites always began with the woman's vow, made to the Sun god for the recovery of the sick or for the safe return of a warrior husband or son from the war trail.

The second day, the sacred woman fasted. The ceremony began. They brought offerings for their prayers for sickness or to settle a family quarrel. Teepees were set up in a circle around the site where they would build the Sun Lodge; they rode their best horses and wore their finest regalia. There was festivity and celebration.

In the final four days, the Shoshoni performed the Sun Dance. The warriors wore breech clouts, and their bodies were painted. Sage was rubbed into their palms, and an attendant filled their pipes. The Sun Pole was a means of sacrifice and thanksgiving to the Sun god for answered prayers. The Shoshoni believed in self-mutilation for religious suffering. Warriors entered to inflict self punishment on

74

their bodies for vows to the Sun god to deliver them from danger, when they were surrounded by the enemy. They believed in self sacrifice for the suffering of the people.

Thongs were attached to the top of the pole. Warriors danced around the Sun Pole with thongs fastened at the top to pegs inserted into slits in their chests for self-affliction. Sometimes, buffalo skulls were inserted by thongs between the ropes and the pegs. Warriors strained to tear the skin, freeing the pegs, or were cut out. They performed the Sun Dance around the centre pole.

The dancers suffered from pain and exhaustion, but continued to dance. Scars on their chest were exhibited as trophies of the ordeal. They wore those scars all of their lives. One type of self-sacrifice was self-torture performed by the warrior by self mutilation. He slashed his arms and legs before going on the war trail. Medicine men prayed for spiritual cleansing. Songs were sung as prayers to heal the sick.

The ritual was performed annually at the Fort Hall Reservation and was held the summer of 1911. In 1912 the Sun Dance was banned, but the order was ignored. They staged the dance on Chief Tendoy's farm in 1913, but the Agent sent word to disband.

The Fort Hall Indians adopted the Native American Church of the Comanche Indians that used Peyote in the ritual of the blood sacrifice of Jesus Christ. It grew to 50,000 members in America, Canada and Mexico by 1966.

The Fort Hall Shoshoni were one of the first Northern Shoshoni tribes to receive horses from the Comanche Indians. After 1700 A.D. Comanche Indians drove horses up to Fort Hall to their Shoshoni cousins, the first Snake bands to acquire horses.

Fort Hall Sketch of Buffalo
Swimming Across the Snake River
Drawing Courtesy of Boise Artist Len Sodenkamp

At first, the Bannock Indians loved to steal horses from the Fort Hall Shoshonis. Horses provided mobility to areas of subsistence. A good war horse was invaluable, as was a fine buffalo horse for hunting and war. A Spanish Mustang served in both roles. A horse drug a travois loaded with goods, infants and tipi outfitting.

Fort Hall Shoshoni met the Bannock Indians as they continued to drift eastward. They first raided and stole horses from the Shoshoni and were considered robbers, but somehow they started trading and got along.

At last, they became friends and allies. The Bannock received horses from the Fort Hall Shoshoni traders. The Fort Hall Shoshoni that dwelled near the fur fort intermarried with the Bannock Indians creating the Shoshoni-Bannock people.

Fort Hall Shoshoni hunted buffalo on their hunting grounds for a time. When they hunted buffalo the Fort Hall Shoshoni were also called Kutsundeka by their peers. Later, they joined the Bear River band and crossed on the Bannock Trail to hunt bison.

Rabbit drives were held to trap jack rabbits. Rabbits also were surrounded and driven into nets and clubbed. It took 200 rabbit skins to make a rabbit fur robe, which gave them a cozy blanket for sleeping in the winter.

Cotton–tail, jack rabbit and snow-shoe rabbits were plentiful and put meat for the table. Rabbits multiply rapidly. Antelope (hutsa) herds ranged into the hundreds. The "desert deer," known for its speed was able to flee instantly from predators.

American Bison
Author Photo

Nathaniel Wyeth organized an expedition and departed Boston, Massachusetts for Oregon Territory to establish a fur trade post. Legend says, Wyeth shot a bison and built Fort Hall where it fell. He built "Fort Hall," a stockade fort 300 miles east of Fort Boise. McKay and Wyeth attended the Green River Rendezvous in 1834. They built Fort Boise and Fort Laramie that year. John McKay chose the site, where John Reed and Donald McKenzie had established Fort Boise. There was a rivalry for the fur trade.

In 1834, Hudson's Bay Company acquired both forts and brought goods from England for trade: beads, blankets, cloth, kettles, guns, knives, pipes, sugar, tobacco, trinkets, utensils and other goods bartered for furs. Six green or yellow beads traded to the Indians for a beaver pelt.

The universal measure of a beaver pelt stretched and dried was a "made beaver" which traded as one point. The trapper looked for a gnawed tree trunk or a beaver dam. A bait stick smeared with the beaver sex gland was hung over a strong metal trap and set inches below water's surface. A chain that ran from the trap to a stake was secured in deeper water. The weight of the heavy trap drowned a caught beaver. Traps were checked and beaver were removed, skinned and bundled

Settlements and teepees sprang up around the fort. Fort Hall Shoshoni lodged around the fur fort. Indians brought furs to the fort in trade for colored beads and other commodities. Mountain men lived off the land, trapped furs and took Indian women for brides.

The Fur Trade in America began about 1811, but by 1840, the beaver had been hunted to near extinction. The beaver trade died out,

1800's Shoshoni Indian Teepees at Fort Hall
Photo Courtesy of Idaho State Historical Society Library

like the buffalo, but remained alive around Fort Hall. As the fur trade slowed, the trappers were attacked by the Indians. When the buffalo vanished, they asked the Indians at Fort Hall, "what happened to all of the buffalo?" Their answer was, "we ate them all."

Chief trader Grant of the Hudson's Bay Company employed expert mountain men to trap. In 1842, he hired Jim Bridger and Peg-Leg Smith to supply Fort Hall with beaver.

Prices dropped in 1848 and the fur trade died off. The California Gold Rush displaced the fur trade. Smith began his own business. During the Fur Trade Era beaver skin top-hats became the rage, but when the beaver trade fell off in 1870, silk top-hats came in.

Wyeth's luck was bad; he wound up selling the Fort Hall fur trade post to the Hudson's Bay Company (H.B.C.). In 1855, it was reported there were some 1500 Shoshoni at Green River, while 700 Shoshoni, 200 Bannock and 300 Sheep-eater lived at Fort Hall.

Shoshoni-Bannock Indians and other tribes traded at Fort Hall, a hub for the fur trade, stage and wagon stops until 1856. The 1854 Ward Massacre and the Indian Wars of 1855 coupled with the erosion of the two forts on the Snake River caused both forts in Idaho Territory to close. The Army camped at Fort Boise, but left later on.

Old Fort Hall later served as an Indian School for Shoshoni-Bannock Indian children. Despite its closure, immigrant wagon trains with their livestock continued to make frequent stops at the fort as they rolled along the Oregon Trail. In 1857, Kit Carson and Jim Bridger and other trappers were attacked by 50 Bannock warriors, while traveling to Fort Hall. A monument was erected there and ruins of the old Fort Hall are still visible today.

The Bannock Indian People
(Photo Courtesy of the Idaho State Historical Society Library)

CHAPTER SEVEN
BANNOCK INDIANS

Passed down through generations was the story of how the ancestors of the Bannock people traversed a long way across the water to arrive on this continent. The Shoshonis called them the *Banaite,* meaning, the "people from below."

Bannocks called themselves, *Pah'ahnuck* (meaning from across the water). A source of the word Bannock was two Shoshoni words, *Bamb* (hair) and (*nack*) backwards motion or *Bampnack,* translated (Bannock). They called themselves *Numa* or "the people" and were taller in stature than the Shoshoni, and light skinned, like the Nez Perce.

Bannock hunters were far ranging across much of what are now Idaho, Montana, Nevada, Oregon, and Wyoming. Millions of bison roamed the Snake River Plain to the Blue Mountains.

Northern Paiute (Numa) lived south and west of the Shoshoni in now Oregon and Nevada. As the buffalo began disappearing from the base of the Blue Mountains, the Paiutes crossed the Snake River and followed behind migrating buffalo north into the western river drainages of present day Idaho. The Boise headwaters begin in the Sawtooth Mountains, flow across Idaho and empty into the Snake and Columbia Rivers then into the Ocean.

Bannock and Shoshoni Indian tribes were both Uto-Aztecan speakers linguistically; their dialects differed some, but helped produce a bond. The Bannock dialect was closer to the Paiute. They had split off as an offshoot of the Northern Paiute and emerged as the

Bannock. They drifted eastward, met the Fort Hall Shoshoni, bonded, and intermarried, creating the Shoshoni-Bannock people.

The romance continues today. Bannock Indians received horses through trade and served as middle men trading ponies to the Cayuse and Nez Perce. It was not uncommon to see Bannock, Nez Perce and Shoshoni camped together. Huge buffalo herds grazed on the Snake River Plain but vanished from Fort Hall after 1840.

The Bannock lodged in extended family bands without a head chief. They may have had a communal leader who was social director of ceremonies, dances, festivals, hunts and war.

In composite bands members were unrelated. The composite bands were loosely formed. These bands seldom numbered over 30. The Bannock, however, did not have societal clans.

Communal drives were held by the Bannock Indians to gather grasshoppers and Mormon crickets for food. The whole village joined in and formed a huge circle around a host of grasshoppers, and closed in on the insects, ensnaring them in center nets. Rich in protein, grasshoppers were pounded in a mortar into pulp, roasted on a stick and eaten or pounded into flour to bake bread.

The Indians formed a huge circle to encompass a herd of antelope. They used brush and rock lanes to drive the herd into the corral, only slaughtered what they needed and freed the rest.

In smaller drives, the band circled the antelope, moving inward until the animal was ensnared in fine netting. An antelope fed the whole family band and the furry hide was prized for its softness. Rabbit and sage hen were also caught using drives. One method of hunting antelope involved a shaman, who used magic to lure an antelope. He hid in the sagebrush and held a bright colored cloth tied to a long stick in the air. The antelope, being a curious animal, came up to the cloth and was shot with a bow and arrow. The Antelope Festival and dance followed the hunt.

The Snakes first described the Bannock as one who always steals horses from me and called them "Robber Indians." The Bannock counted coup stealing Shoshoni horses. Bannocks were horse-mounted thanks to the Shoshoni, through theft and then in trade.

Horses provided mobility to areas of subsistence. A good Spanish Mustang horse was invaluable as a war horse or buffalo horse. A horse could drag a travois loaded with goods and tipi.

The Bannock Indians wore breech clouts, leggings and moccasins during warfare and painted their faces with colorful war paint. The Bannock also painted their favorite war horses for battle. One famous mark was a black handprint on the horse. They were strong warriors in battle armed with lance, bow and arrows or rifles.

The communal buffalo jump was an unusual technique of hunting. Lanes were built on a plateau with rock barriers along the sides forming a barrier. A shaman whooped and waved a blanket; the herd grazing near the cliff stampeded over the edge to their death to be processed into meat and hides in butchering stations.

Chief Tahgee and Chief Buffalo Horn led parties to the Upper Missouri to hunt the buffalo. Buffalo hunters left Fort Hall under the direction of the hunt leader. The Bannock and Shoshonis rode through the Tahgee Pass along the "Great Bannock Trail" and continued over the Continental Divide to the Upper Missouri.

Bannock Warriors
(Photo Courtesy of the Idaho State Historical Society Library)

Bannock hunters accompanied their Shoshoni allies on horseback to the Upper Missouri to hunt buffalo, joined by other tribes as protection from ambush. Hunting parties rode in large groups, because they were vulnerable to bands of marauding Blackfeet Indians, who would attack at any time to steal their horses. The Bannocks were fierce in battle and engaged the Blackfeet in war. They were good hunters and fierce warriors, who took Blackfeet scalps. The Bannock Indians were ready to fight any Blackfeet. They were called Blackfeet Indians from walking across the burned prairie. Oft times the Bannock war-party was the victor. Bannocks stole horses. They scalped and counted coup. Back in camp the victory dance or scalp dance was performed. Many guns and scalps were taken.

They delighted in stealing horses from other tribes, building up large herds. Wealth was measured in the number of horses they owned. Raids were made on enemy bands to retrieve stolen horses. Bannocks were "hunters and gatherers" for subsistence. They moved around gathering food in four rhythmic seasonal cycles. The Bannock women were called "Digger Indians" as they dug the edible roots and gathered fleshy fruits, leaves, berries, nuts and seeds.

The Bannock banded together with the Shoshoni and fished along the Snake River below Shoshone Falls for Chinook. Schools of fish amassed that failed to climb the falls. They fished through the summer along the Snake River, past the confluence of the Boise, Payette and Weiser Rivers to the Salmon River. They employed harpoons and nets, and stone weirs across streams to slow the salmon. Salmon was their main staple. They lived on fish, roots and game.

Shoshone Falls, Idaho
Fishing Area of the Bannock Indians
(Photo Courtesy of Wikimedia.org)

John C. Freemont recorded seeing Salmon-eaters fishing at Shoshone Falls in Idaho. Early autumn they migrated south to pick pinion pine-nuts. Bands of Bannock and Nez Perce met to celebrate. Teepees were set up in a large circle of both tribes. They danced and celebrated in unison. Bannocks traded buffalo robes to the Nez Perce for deerskin war shirts; horses, beads, wives and other goods.

The women made war shirts for the men of two deer skins and made dresses the same way, but of two elk skins. The men wore a breech clout to cover their loins. Leggings were worn from the hip to the ankle and moccasins. Women wore legging to the knee.

In early autumn, Bannock and Shoshoni families moved up to the hills onto the Camas Prairie. Women dug the camas root and ground it in mortar and pestles into flour for Indian bread.

In late autumn they returned to Fort Hall to prepare for the buffalo hunt. Hunters targeted antelope, bear, buffalo, deer, rabbit, and brought game back for the band. Parties hunted antelope and deer on horseback in the fall, when they were meaty. In the winter, the Bannock Indians winter camped with the Fort Hall Shoshonis.

Sometimes the Crow were friendly with the Bannock and traded with them and other times they fought. The Bannocks and the Flatheads were normally allies, but sometimes squabbles occurred over horse theft.

Raids were led by a band chief. A ritual was held before a raid. The warriors held a buffalo robe; others beat it and chanted. The people gave supplies and food for the hunt and wished them good luck. The Bannock Indians traded directly with Jim Bridger and Captain Benjamin L. Bonneville. Rarely did they invite white men to hunt buffalo with them. The Bannock Indians normally disliked palefaces trespassing on their lands. The Bannocks did not have much sympathy for the palefaces, nor did they fear them.

Fort Hall Shoshoni were normally friendly to the white man. Most of the Bannock Indians at Fort Hall were mean and generally did not much like the white man and would rather raid the whites' horses than befriend them. They expected a paleface entering their camp to observe their customs and smoke the pipe with them; if the whites ignored these policies, they might fight them.

Horse thieves, the fierce and warlike Bannock were disliked by white people. When the white man arrived, they confused the Bannock with the Paiute Indians, farther west. Immigrants visited Fort Hall and estimated the Bannocks' numbers to be over 1,000, and the Shoshoni Indians they hunted and wintered with at nearly 1500.

Marie was an Iowa Sioux Indian born in a teepee on the banks of the Missouri River, who married Pierre Dorian, Jr., a French-Sioux Indian cross. Wilson Price Hunt in St. Louis needed an interpreter in 1811. Pierre Jr. spoke Sioux and signed on with Wilson Price Hunt in St. Louis as interpreter, and brought his family.

August 1804, Pierre met Lewis and Clark on the Missouri through his father. The Hunt Party left St. Louis, paddled up the Missouri in dugout canoes and reached the Green River Valley where they traded with the Shoshoni, hunted buffalo and jerked two tons of meat. Crossing the Hobart River Valley Basin they sank their dugouts in the Snake and crossed the Continental Divide on horse-back. They rode southwest to Jackson's Hole and hiked out of the Tetons. Four traders stayed to trap beaver; Crow Indians killed one of the trappers.

Paiute Indians in front of their wickiup shelter.
(Photo Courtesy of Wikimedia.org)

Two Shoshonis guided them across the Snake River, up Fall Creek over Teton Pass and again crossed the divide. They rode horses to Pierre's Hole and floated in dugouts down the north fork of the Snake to Henry's Fork. They lost canoes and a man drowned at Caldron Lynn.

Hiking three days without water on the Snake River Canyon into now Idaho, Marie suffered from exhaustion and thirst. They reached Hagerman Valley, and found precious drinking water. Hunt's party had made it over the Rockies! Near Eagle, Idaho they met Shoshoni Indians who shared fresh puppy meat with them.

Pierre traded the Indians for a much needed horse and later had to dismount and surrender the horse to Marie and the boys. Indians scoffed at some tribes' eating dog meat, others considered it a delicacy. Spent horses were sometimes eaten in the absence of food. Even Lewis and Clark ate horse flesh at "Colt Killed Camp."

Marie and Sacajawea (two famous women), once met briefly, in 1811, as the Manual Lisa Party overtook the Hunt party. The party split into three groups led by Hunt, McKenzie and Crooks who reached Astoria, May 11, 1812. Their fur shipments to Great Britain were jeopardized by the War of 1812. In 1813, Pierre and Marie returned to the mouth of the Boise River working for Reed in the Astoria group. Reed's post was erected on the eastside of the Snake.

La Chapelle, Le Clerc, Dorian and Rezner lived in a cabin (lean-to) Reed built to hunt the beaver. He abandoned the original Fort Boise (cabin) since unruly Indians often demanded guns. In 1814, a band of warring Bannock burned down the abandoned cabin and continued down the Boise whooping and chanting war-songs.

92

Marie was skinning beaver at Reed's cabin, 15 miles east of the burned cabin, north of the Boise River near what is now Notus, Idaho. A woman informed her that warring Dog-ribs (Bannocks) were coming up river.

Marie rode up stream to find Pierre and camped overnight and the next day because of bad weather. Seeing a Bannock smoke signal, Marie stayed there another day. Table Rock, called "Ala-Kush-pa," is a plateau Indians used to send smoke signals.

Marie discovered Le Clerc just barely alive. He told her of the massacre; she hoisted him up onto her horse, but he fell off. Approaching the cabin, Marie saw Indians gallop off on horseback.

Le Clerc died; she buried him under snow and brush. Marie reached the cabin and saw her husband's scalped and mutilated body.

The children were hungry and cold and had not eaten in days. Marie built a fire, returned to the cabin, armed with a knife and tomahawk and saw wolves eating their kill. She scared them off and found fresh fish in the cabin, hurried back, and cooked the fish. Marie must care for her boys alone.

She mounted her horse and crossed the Snake River to begin a long trek to Fort Astoria. Marie led her horse over the snow-covered Blue Mountains, located an overhang and built a fire; they were snug and warm and lived on berries, nuts and rabbits.

Her resources ran out. Marie had to resort to killing her horse for food in order to survive and trudged westward, her papoose in a cradleboard strapped to her back. She held little Baptist's hand. Marie was snow-blind and exhausted as they reached the Umatilla Indians, who rescued them.   ^^◇^^

93

Wavoka, Paiute Medicine Man
of the Dream Shirt Religion
Courtesy of Wikimedia.org

Bannock Girl Carrying Firewood
(Photo Courtesy of the Idaho
State Historical Society Library)

In 1872, Smohalla, a Nez Perce prophet, proclaimed that Indians would rise up from the dead and drive the white-eyes out of the land, initiating the Dreamer's Religion.

Wavoca, a Nevada Paiute holy man, white men called Jack Wilson, probably used peyote and had a vision of immortal warriors in Ghost Shirts dancing in a circle invincible to white man's bullets.

"Ghost Shirt Religion" frenzy spread and hundreds of Indians rallied to fight the white man for redemption. Word traveled fast of the Ghost Dance to Fort Hall and the Plains, reaching the Sioux.

In 1890, Sioux braves did the Ghost Dance in their sacred shirts one evening, let go war-whoops, shot off rifles, and danced around a huge bonfire late in the night at Wounded Knee which scared the settlers in settlements nearby.

The Army rode to Chief Sitting Bull's cabin the next day and pulled Chief Sitting Bull from his sleeping robes and fired. The old chief tried to flee and was shot dead. It was the passing of an era.

After the Ghost Dance 300 Sioux Indian Ghost dancers of all ages were massacred near Wounded Knee Creek by the 7th U.S. Cavalry, infantry and Buffalo soldiers. They were equipped with Cannons and Gatling guns.

Wavoka's dream of the Ghost Shirts became a nightmare. Many Sioux fled into the mountains. A large number of Indians also lost their lives in the freezing snow. The massacre was protested.

Trade-blankets were worn after the arrival of the white man and fur forts. A blanket Indian was an Indian who refused to accept the ways of the palefaces and wore the blanket in protest.

Shoshoni Chief Pocatello
with Peace Medals
Photo Courtesy of Wikimedia.org

CHAPTER EIGHT
BEAR RIVER SHOSHONI

Bear Lake was divided by the Idaho-Utah Territory border just northeast of the Great Salt Lake ten miles west of the Wyoming Territorial border. Bear Lake Shoshoni country encompassed all three territories.

The Bear River Shoshoni Indians lodged and fished the large freshwater Bear Lake and the Bear River drainage of Idaho. There was an abundance of salmon and trout. They caught salmon, mountain whitefish, cutthroat and steelhead. Bear Lake had a large amount of wildlife. The Shoshoni hunted antelope, bear, cougar, deer, elk, moose and other wild game.

There were large hawks and eagles. The egret, heron, pelican and other wading birds fished there. Ducks and geese flocked to the lake. As hunters and gatherers, they ate buffalo, deer, rabbits, squirrels, sage hens, fish, ants and many other animals for food.

Shoshoni lineage passed through the father's line. Polygamy was common among the Shoshoni and was practiced in marriage from their prehistory. A man marrying an Indian bride also took her little sisters for wives. They all dwelled in the one lodge.

Non-related wives dwelled in a separate lodge. If a woman wanted more than one husband, she married her husband's younger brothers. Later, the Shoshoni became monogamous. If the wife died, the husband married her sister; if a woman's husband died, she married her husband's brother. In the case of a death, there was open mourning. The deceased's belongings were burned, his house torn down; if a band leader died, camp was moved.

The rite-of-passage for a brave to become a man was the vision quest. He ventured out alone in the wild until he received a vision. Animals in nature were a part of their belief system. If the brave envisioned an eagle, for example, it became the young brave's spirit guide through his lifetime. The Shoshoni believed in dreams and visions and to them all material animate or inanimate had life, like the sun, moon, and stars, a belief called animism.

Atlatl is an Aztec Indian word for spear thrower, a throwing device, about two feet long with finger-loops on the throwing end and a bone spur to engage the end of the spear. A weight was added for momentum. Using the devise, the spear and atlatl were held in one hand. The dart was thrust to increase distance and speed up to 100 yards, to kill mammoth elephant, bison-bison and other mammals.

Bow and arrows date back thousands of years for hunting. Shoshoni crafted fine bows and arrows of juniper, oak, osage and yew. Plains Indians practiced wrapping rattlesnake skin around a bow to protect it and for popular adornment. Bowstrings were made from animal gut, called sinew.

Arrows were fashioned from willow or any of the above woods and tipped with arrow heads made of bone, stone, or wood. The shaft was heated and straightened, then smoothed and polished for an arrow, using grooved stone abraders, smoothers and lastly, polishers. Eagle, hawk, owl or wild turkey feathers were used to fletch an arrow. The Shoshoni caught hawks and eagles and kept them in stick cages for their feathers.

Plains Indians were expert flint knappers. They started with a stone core and struck pieces of from it. These pieces were shaped by

Bear River in Southeastern Idaho
Haunt of the Bear River Shoshonis
Photo Courtesy of Wikipedia.org

pressure and percussion. Indians flint knapped (chipped) arrowheads from chert, flint, or obsidian and inserted them into a slit at the shaft end, glued with pitch and wrapped the point with sinew.

They made lithic tools: arrowheads, gravers, hide scrapers, knives, shaft scrapers and spearheads were flaked from basalt, chert, or obsidian. Hammers, shovels, and tomahawks took much larger cores. Awls, burins and sewing needles were crafted from bone

Leather quivers made of cougar skin slung over the shoulder, held their arrows. To deflect arrows, war shields were made of tough buffalo hide from the neck region. The thickest part of the skin was used for war shields for protection. The wet circular piece was dried over a pit fire. Holes burned around the edge were used to lash the hide to the frame, made of a sapling tied in a circle for a shield with eagle feathers attached. War shields held sacred power of the gods.

Personal symbols were painted on the shields, teepees and sometimes clothing. The warrior was outfitted with bow, arrows, knife, lance, tomahawk, war shield and rifle. Prehistoric knives were flaked from chert with bone or wood handles. Scalp knives were wooden handled butcher knives bartered from trade forts.

Shoshoni scouts located wild bison herds to hunt. Hunting buffalo was a communal project. The whole village took part in the hunt. Hunters shot the wild bison to be processed into meat and hides at butchering stations. Women scraped the skins and tanned the hides. They cooked the meat for a great feast.

Skins were made into clothes, moccasins and teepee covers. Intestines made bindings. Horns became spoons and the hooves, glue. Porcupine tails made hair brushes. Buckskin bags were used for seeds. Salmon skins stored pemmican. Combs were carved bone. Men and women wore bear claw or elk tooth necklaces. White man's Tobacco tin cone lids made fine jingle bells worn on dresses.

Pottery came from river clay and baskets were woven of grasses. The Indians made an industry using natural materials. Nature provided them with all the materials that they needed.

For thousands of years the Shoshoni were a pedestrian Indians. Shortly after 1700 A.D., they became equestrian Indians and traveled on horseback on their seasonal rounds. Horses pulled goods with the travois. Horses were used to hunt and for war. Horse races were popular. The buffalo and horse changed their culture.

The Bear River Shoshoni probably received horses through trade with the Eastern or Fort Hall Shoshoni and became a horse community with a buffalo based economy. Extended family bands became horse-mounted and moved easily behind the buffalo herds.

Annually, the Bear Lake Shoshoni hosted a trade fair at their summer encampment held at Bear Lake in Idaho Territory. They traded horses, furs, wives, bows, arrows and arrowheads.

They sang, danced, told stories, played games, raced horses and gambled. Young couples found romance. Chief Washakie and his Wind and Green River Eastern Goshiute Shoshoni came from western Wyoming Territory to Bear Lake for the festivities.

Donald McKenzie of the Hudson's Bay Company crossed over the Blue Mountains with a large trapping brigade. He left six Iroquois Indians at the second Fort Boise with food, gear and traps. McKenzie took a brigade in boats, up the Snake River. He dropped off brigades of trappers at outposts, reaching the Bear River.

Photo believed to be Chief Pocatello
Photo Courtesy of the Idaho State
Historical Society Library

Nathaniel Wyeth built Fort Hall just north of Bear Lake, 125 miles north of Salt Lake. The trading post had four cabins surrounded by Indian lodges. Covered wagon trains stopped at Fort Hall.

Mountain man Peg-Leg Smith became involved in human trafficking and was a party to capturing Indian children he traded to the Spanish colonists for horses. Peg-Leg joined Ute Indian Chief Walkara and Jim Breckenridge in the horse business. He built up a huge herd of horse stock from California around 1840. Peg-Leg Smith was described as a rugged, fleshy and a rough looking character with a wooden leg. It seems Smith was in a horrid accident and had to remove his own leg with a Bowie knife.

Smith chose a site close to Bear Lake as base for his beaver operations located on an old fur trade route on the Bear River in Shoshoni Territory. The trade route became the cut-off that surpassed Fort Bridger and Fort Hall, the emigrant road to California and Oregon.

Traders, Indians and covered wagons came to trade along the Montana trail, with regular stops by the Overland Stage and Wells Fargo stage lines. After that, traders and many Indians came for trade. Smith owned cattle and horses and supplied the miners and emigrants along the trail with supplies, becoming quite wealthy.

The Union Pacific rails ran across Shoshoni territory and the junction to Oregon and Colorado was at Pocatello Station, followed by the Utah and Northern Railroad. Rails reached from Granger, Wyoming to Huntington, Oregon and supplied Boise by 1884. Buffalo hunters killed thousands of bison left to rot; the railroad hauled hides at a profit.

A legend of great bravery on the part of Widzhebu, who would later give birth to Pocatello, was told among the Shoshoni people. An Assiniboine war party attacked a small group of Grouse Creek Shoshonis on Raft River in autumn and captured the women and children. Widzhebu (Cunning Eye) her two year old daughter and niece were stolen by the Assiniboine warriors. Widzhebu was slowed by her baby that was due .On the trail, the warriors did a scalp dance and displayed the scalp of her brother on a pole. They made poor Widzhebu watch the ritual.

An old warrior guarded them while the band hunted near the Bannock Range southwest of Fort Hall. The captives lagged behind him. When the time was right the niece escaped, ran and hid, never to be seen again. The party continued to move on and traveled north into Montana country hundreds of miles to reach their village.

Widzhebu was given to a brave, who treated her cruelly. He blamed for the loss of the slave girl and pulled her papoose from the cradleboard, and silenced her. Then, he chastised Widzhebu. She learned he had a wife and four year old daughter. A captive woman from Raft River told her that the other wife planned to kill her.

Widzhebu did women's work. She cooked and gathered firewood and went out daily with the four year old girl to gather wood. One day her Assiniboine husband went hunting, while Widzhebu and the girl went for firewood. She took the girl's life with the hatchet. Widzebu had been digging a cave in the river bank, in secret that was now big enough to crawl into and hide. Widzhebu had an escape plan and was ready to enact it.

Widzhebu hid in the cave. They looked for her for three days before giving up. On the evening of the third day, she began the long trek homeward to Raft River and ran night and day without stopping. Just as the food ran out, Widzhebu reached an Assiniboine grave. On it lay a knife, bow and arrows and a food offering for the deceased. he was famished by then and took the bow, arrows, knife, and the dried meat and ate it, and continued her journey.

Widzhebu walked for days and survived the 600 mile trek across the Montana plains, the Continental Divide and began to see the mountains of home before she finally arrived at her destination on Raft River. Some Shoshonis directed her to the main camp. She was greeted by her mother, father and husband. Widzhebu gave birth to a baby daughter; four years later she had a son named Pocatello.

Pocatello was born around 1815 on the Raft River which empties into the Snake River. His given name was Tanaioza (pronounced Dono Oso) or Buffalo Robe. Pocatello's mother, Widzhebu was a Grouse Creek Shoshoni Indian and his father was a Flathead Indian named Cornell.

Pocatello is not a Shoshoni word, but it may have been a Flathead name. Pocatello grew to be 5' 10" tall, a strong leader, who became chief of 300 Bear Lake Shoshoni Indians. His territory included Bear Lake, Bear River Valley and Raft River north to the Snake and the Great Salt Lake to the south. The California Trail routes: the Fort Hall, Hudspeth, Salt Lake and Oregon routes all cut through Pocatello's territory. Pocatello lodged between the junction of the California Trail and the Salt Lake Road. He rebelled against the hated white intruders that trespassed on their lands.

U.S. Army Colonel Patrick E. Conner and his company of 3rd California Voluntary Infantry Regiment were ordered to Utah to protect the Overland Mail Route and keep peace in the region.

Settlers killed game where his people usually hunted and used the water holes for their livestock, exhausting the supply. Cattle grazed grasses down to nothing and game could not forage. Settlers destroyed seeds the Shoshoni gathered for food. Pocatello hated to see his people starve during cold winters, so he camped near Indian Agent Brigham Young's camp, who gave him food and supplies.

In 1857, Pocatello rose to power and greatness in his band as a leader. Pocatello was a silent chief considered to be a hostile. In 1858, General Johnston arrived in Utah Territory with his troops. Even President Abraham Lincoln had heard of Chief Pocatello.

Palefaces trespassed on Shoshoni lands and in 1859 there were numerous attacks along the Bear River, Cache Valley, Hudspeth Cutoff, City of Rocks and Massacre Rocks all in Pocatello's territory.

A small train was attacked on July 26, 1859 at Twin Springs. In 1859, the Shepherd train was massacred south of Twin Springs. The following day, Snakes raided wagons at the Hudspeth Cutoff.

On August 31, 1859, Shoshonis massacred the Miltimore family in the American Falls vicinity. The Snakes made a series of raids on trains in eastern Idaho Territory. In 1859, two of Pocatello's warriors were killed by white men; he retaliated and sent out a war party that killed six emigrants.

In 1859, Chief Pocatello rode to Lieutenant Gay's camp. Gay arrested Pocatello and put him in the guard house. Major Lynde, Gay's commanding officer, released the Chief for lack of evidence.

An unidentified member of Pocatello's band
Photo Courtesy of Legends of America.com

Shoshoni Chief Pocatello appealed to Eastern Shoshoni Chief Washakie to join him in war on the palefaces. Washakie was a peace chief and declined making a permanent enemy of Chief Pocatello.

June 23, 1860, a Shoshoni band attacked an Army road party in Malheur County, Oregon. October 16, 1860 renegades massacred the Utter Party west of Castle Butte in Owyhee County.

Palefaces trespassed on Shoshone lands, and in retaliation, Indians attacked the intruders. In 1860, a train was attacked in the City of Rocks. That fall, Shoshoni massacred the Utter train on the Snake and attacked Soda Springs in 1861. They stole livestock from the Harrison train in the City of Rocks.

August 9, 1862 emigrants traveled west. The Adams, Wilson and Kennedy trains followed the Smart wagon west. One half mile from Massacre Rocks, a war-party ambushed the Smart and Adam's train, massacred settlers, stole livestock and burned their wagons.

In the Utah war, parties attacked the farmers. War parties killed white men, women and children and scalped them. Pocatello's band captured women and children for slaves and wives. They burned the wagons and stole livestock. Slaves were captured in Indian fashion and they had taken captives from enemy tribes for years

The army hoped to establish a military garrison in the Boise Valley, an extension of Fort Vancouver. Fort Boise was built in 1863 to protect the emigrants and miners. General Crook made his headquarters there. The Cavalry could be dispensed any time.

The Shoshonis had gathered for the traditional warm dance in Bear Hunter's village in January of 1863 to welcome the spring to come early and bless the bands with warm weather and abundance.

In 1863, the Bannock killed a white man, rumored to be an emigrant near Brigham City. Chief Snag and two braves came in to Brigham City to answer charges they had held a white captive, but the three Indians were shot down in the street at Bannock City by miners. Meanwhile, Chief Bear Hunter's warriors did a war dance around the home of Mormon Bishop Preston Thomas, demanding wheat. The next day, Bear Hunter returned and was told the soldiers were near. Hearing that he could be killed, Bear Hunter stated that the soldiers might be killed, also. The chief rode to warn his people.

Colonel Conner rode to Bear River with an order for the Shoshoni to turn over the Indians responsible, but they would not turn in the culprits. Chiefs Pocatello had left the previous day prior to Conner's attack and took Sagwitch and other willing Shoshoni with him to safety. Chief Bear Hunter and other sub-chiefs refused to join Pocatello and vacate camp, taking Colonel Conner's demands lightly.

Colonel Conner stated that he planned to take no prisoners of those that resisted. His plan was to chastise the Utah Indians for their wrong-doings. Colonel Conner marched at night from Salt Lake, in order to provide the element of surprise. Two cavalry units marched at once. The town of Preston, Idaho heard of the approaching troops.

Conner left Salt Lake by nightfall. At dawn, January 29, 1863, they swam their horses across the icy cold Bear River, one mile south of Bear Hunter's camp nestled in a ravine. The Soldiers appeared, dismounted and the fighting began.

One hundred Bannock warriors fled to the hills. The fighting lasted four hours. Bear Hunter and 250 Indians were estimated dead, including women and children. The Army lost 23. Soldiers burned 75 teepees, captured 175 horses, and found 1,000 bushels of stolen wheat and left some for the Indians. Conner was promoted to Brig. General.

A rumor reached them that Pocatello and his warriors were seeking a fight with General Conner and his troops, but when the Army answered, the Indians rode to the hills. Meanwhile, the Bannock Indians had moved into the Wind River Mountains.

After the Bear River Massacre, Colonel Conner attempted to capture Chief Pocatello, but to no avail. Chief Pocatello had escaped to the Green River region of Wyoming.

The Bear River Massacre stopped the Indian attacks. Wagon trains crossed into Oregon unscathed. After the massacre chiefs Pocatello, San Pitch and their band were exonerated.

Conner rode to Fort Hall to remove any remaining hostiles. He left Salt Lake by nightfall with his Cavalry. At the Snake River Ferry, he came upon 17 Shoshoni lodges.

They were peaceable, so Conner gave out gifts to the Shoshoni. If peaceable, he told them they would not meet the fate of those at Bear River.

Chief Winnemucca promised Agent John Burche of Nevada in May of 1863, that he would persuade Chief Pashego (*Pas-se-quah*) of the Nevada and Idaho Bannock to attend a conference. Agent Burche met with the chiefs on the Humboldt River and Pashego, who promised no more attacks on the palefaces, if the Indians were left alone promised to keep the peace. Chief Pocatello sent word via Washakie that he was ready to talk peace. Chiefs of nine Shoshoni bands, including Chiefs Pocatello and Sanpitch, except Sagwitch, signed the Box Elder Treaty at Brigham City, Utah July 30, 1863.

An emigrant wagon train 40 miles west of Fort Hall was later attacked by Indians. Conner's Bear River massacre had made an impression and Indian attacks on wagon trains had slowed to a stop. Meanwhile, the Indians left to hunt the buffalo.

In October of 1864, General Patrick E. Conner arrested Chief Pocatello and transported him to Fort Douglas in Utah and charged him with theft. Pocatello was a brave leader of his people, feared by the military, Indian agents and settlers.

Pocatello stood up to Army officers. General Conner knew that Chief Pocatello was responsible for the recent raids in eastern Idaho Territory and planned to hang Pocatello.

Utah Indian Agent O.H. Irish telegraphed President Abraham Lincoln and apprised him of Conner's intentions. President Lincoln was working on a peaceful resolve between the immigrants and the Indians.

When Lincoln learned of the actions against the chief, he directed the Secretary of War to telegraph General Conner not to execute Chief Pocatello. General Conner released Pocatello.

The Shoshoni Indians went to the Fort Hall Reservation. August 21, 1867, Governor Ballard spoke to the chiefs:

"Now, are you willing to relinquish your title to all of the country you have claimed provided the government of the United States secures to you and your children, and to such other friendly Indians as maybe induced to go there on, the sole ownership of said reservation forever, supply you with subsistence until you can raise sufficient food for yourselves and furnish you an agent, teachers, books, implements of husbandry, etc."

111

Gen. Patrick E. Conner
(Courtesy of Wikipedia.org)

President Abraham Lincoln
Photo Courtesy of
Wikimedia.org

Chief Tah-gee spoke, *"I thought when the white people came to Soda Springs and built homes and put soldiers in them, it was to protect my people, but now they are all gone, and I do not know where to go, or what to do."* The chief continued. *"The white people have come into my country, and have not asked my consent. And why have no persons talked to me before? I have never killed white people who were passing through my country. All the Bannock will obey me and be good, but the Sheep-eaters are not my people and I cannot be responsible for them. I will answer for the Bannock. The buffalo do not come as far south now as formerly, so we go further to the north to hunt them. The white people have scared them away."*

∧∧◇∧∧

After the massacre, Chief Pocatello liked to walk with various friends and their dogs just enjoying them. Chief Pocatello came out of his shell and even began to make friends among the white people.

Chief Pocatello wore a discarded colonel's coat and a sword presented to him by an officer. The aging Chief had been ill and in October of 1884, he was taken to the Snake River bottoms in Idaho, where he died.

When Pocatello passed, he was buried in his regalia. Chief Pocatello instructed his people that he was to be buried in a huge spring with an unknown depth beneath the American Falls Reservoir.

The Chief was to be interred in his garb and Army coat, with his bow and arrows, guns and knives all tied to his body. All 18 of his horses were to be slaughtered and buried with his corpse for Pocatello to use in the spiritual afterlife.

113

Wind River Shoshonis
Courtesy of Wikimedia.org

CHAPTER NINE
EASTERN SHOSHONI

A band of Shoshoni had split from their Wind River Shoshoni people, circa 1500 A.D. They became nomadic and traveled southward into present day northern Texas, where they became known as the Comanche Indians and were called the "Horse Indians."

The U.S. Army referred to the Wyoming Territory Green and Wind River Goshute Shoshoni, as the Eastern Shoshoni. They were hunters and gatherers called hunters of the buffalo (Buffalo eaters). They hunted the buffalo with the use of the horse. The two bands numbered around 2,000 Goshutes (cat-tail eaters). They dwelled in the Green and Wind River Valleys in the Wind River Mountains of Western Wyoming from Utah and Wyoming into Colorado Territory. The Wind River and Bighorn Mountains were their hunting grounds.

The Eastern Shoshonis were the most eastern band of the Shoshoni tribe and ranged from the Bear River near the mouth of Smith Fork on the west (Idaho), from south pass on the headwaters of the North Platte River on the east, on the south as far as Brown's Hole (Green River), and the Wood River on the north (Wyoming). In 1863, Shoshoni lands spanned 44 million acres, from Salt Lake Valley to the lofty Teton Mountains into Yellowstone National Park.

Born shortly after 1800, Washakie was the son of a Salish Flathead and a Lemhi Shoshoni mother. He was just a papoose when Lewis and Clark lodged spent the winter of 1804 with the Mandans. A strong warrior Washakie rode among the Blackfeet, Crow and Sioux scaring their horses with his rattle that sounded like a rattle-snake. Their horses reared, or bolted, and threw the riders.

Wind River, on the Wind River Reservation
Photo Courtesy of Wikipedia.org

Washakie became chief of the Green and Wind River Goshutes of the Eastern Shoshoni in 1850. Chief Washakie had many sub-chiefs and was a powerful voice among the Shoshoni. Washakie was a brave warrior and war chief.

The great Chief Washakie had influence over many Indians. It is hard to believe that Washakie warred against the white man in 1862 attacking immigrant wagon trains and stage stops instead it was probably Ute Chief Kanache or Pocatello that assaulted them.

Washakie's daughter married Jim Bridger, who lived among the Indians. Jim married three Indian wives in their tradition. A Flathead woman bore him three children. His second wife was Ute. Jim's third wife was the daughter of Chief Washakie. She bore two children; one daughter was a student at the Whitman Mission School.

A legendary story was told about Jim Bridger. A small band of angry Blackfeet Indians was in hot pursuit of Bridger. They disliked him trapping animals in their territory. Bridger retreated; his horse lathered and ran in a full gallop. He rode for his life to the fort. Bridger managed to stay alive, kept his scalp, but caught an arrow in the back. He survived three years with the arrow-head in his backbone. Finally, Marcus Whitman removed it without anesthetic.

Jim trapped for two decades; he built "Fort Bridger" with a partner, Louis Vasquez on Black's Fork of the Green River, in present day Wyoming in 1843.

Fort Bridger became a major way station on the Oregon Trail for trade with the Indians and mountain men. Jim scouted for the U.S. Army, Railroad, and Overland Stage Company. He quarreled with the LDS in Salt Lake, but sold them his fort.

Washakie (center) Eastern Shoshoni Village
Photo Courtesy of the Smithsonian Institute

Fort Washakie 1892 with Shoshoni Chief Washakie extending arm.
(Photo Courtesy of Wikimedia.org)

Wagon trains poured west along the Oregon Trail. Washakie met the white man in peace and did not war with them. Instead Washakie was a peacemaker and befriended the immigrants.

A favorite legend of the Shoshoni Indians is the story of the Chief Washakie's white son. This is a true story that occurred in Wyoming Territory, in 1859. Hiram and his sister ran away from Fort Bridger to play with Indian children. Crossing a meadow, Hiram was taken captive by an Indian on horseback, the girl escaped. The Shoshoni warrior took the boy to the Shoshoni village and teepee of Chief Washakie, presenting the boy to him.

Washakie was delighted with the boy and adopted him. The chief gave him four ponies, dressed him in Indian regalia, and the women braided his hair. The chief loved Hiram and raised him for five years. Washakie warned the boy to stay away from whites, but one evening Hiram mounted his pony and rode down into Salt Lake.

The boy was discovered sleeping in a barn, wrapped in a bearskin robe wearing a breech-clout, leggings, beaded deerskin shirt and long blonde braids. Hiram was reunited with his family.

Hiram learned that his sister, for fear that Indians would take her, had been placed on a wagon train for the Whitman Mission and never heard from again.

The family traveled along the Platte River, where large herds of buffalo could be seen in Nebraska Territory traveling to St. Louis. Later, he and his friend Felix Bridger, son of Jim Bridger served as water carriers on a wagon-train to Santa Fe.

As a young man, Hiram went out on his own, finding work at a settlement in La Veta, Colorado for Colonel Francisco. Chief

Kanache and 1,000 Ute warriors surrounded the settlement. Hiram became a hero by riding out at night and bringing back the Cavalry from Fort Lyon, on the Arkansas River.

Eastern Shoshoni Indians attended the Trade Fair that the Boise Shoshonis held to trade goods and horses. They also held trade fairs. Furs, horses, bows and arrows and other goods were bartered. They danced, gambled and told stories. Indians assembled from all around.

In 1866, a Blackfoot war party took horses from the Eastern Shoshoni. Chief Washakie tracked them north for 600 miles. He retrieved the horses, and took enemy scalps.

Counting coup was a favorite of the Shoshoni. They enjoyed going on the war trail on a moonlit night and stealing into a Crow encampment to take a string of horses. The Crow too loved to take Shoshoni horses to avenge their losses.

Ten years earlier, Chief Washakie led a war party against the Crow Indians. Washakie loved to battle. Washakie was known for his prowess in warfare and his number of scalps. They fought hard for several days until the fighting slowed down.

Chief Washakie and Crow Indian Chief, Big Robber agreed to fight a duel on horseback over the hunting grounds in Wind River Valley. Washakie and Big Robber rode toward each other. Washakie stayed low and took his shot killing Chief Big Robber.

Washakie cut out his heart and ate some of it as power over the Chief. The Chief paraded back and forth with the heart hoisted on the point of his lance until after the Shoshoni performed the victory dance to show respect for Big Robber's courage.

The mighty Crow watched in awe. The fierce Crow tribe never attacked the Eastern Shoshoni again; the site of the duel was called Crow-heart Butte for the famous battle. A Wyoming historical marker was erected on the butte to denote the famous duel.

Washakie was amicable to the fur trapper, pioneer, and a friend to Kit Carson. Chief Washakie assisted weary immigrants in fording swollen Streams and recover stray cows.

The Chief demanded that American churches, hospitals, and schools should be of good quality for the Indian people in Wyoming. Washakie chose to build his home in his beloved Wind River Mountains with plenty of food and good drinking water.

In 1868, the Eastern Shoshoni Indians were placed on the Wind River Indian Reservation in the Wind River Mountains of western Wyoming. In 1869, when Fort Brown was established in Lander, Wyoming Chief Washakie met the Army in friendship.

Chief Washakie has been described as quite tall, having a fair complexion, muscular, a powerful built, and a dignified carriage. He was a man that was aware of his position. Washakie was fond of the pomp and ceremony in dealing with the white man.

Washakie was a proponent of rights for the red man. He spoke out against the white man killing the buffalo. He told of the white man's livestock eating the grass in the meadows where their horses would normally graze and killing the game that was food for the Indian. Washakie complained of the trappers depleting the furs that the Indians used for their clothing.

In 1871, the government issued a proclamation to kill off the buffalo and execute the Indians transition onto the reservations.

Buffalo in the Tetons
Photo Courtesy of Ned Eddins

The Eastern Shoshoni began to suffer and starve for lack of buffalo and game animals to feed them. Chief Washakie had been a friend to the white man, but their government had let him down.

Washakie served as an emissary of good will for Indians that resisted the reservation. He voluntarily worked in helping various bands transition onto reservations peacefully. He rode to the camp of Pocatello in 1863 in order to persuade him to come in for peace talks before the Bear River Massacre. After warning the Bannock and Shoshoni, Washakie led his people to Fort Bridger and safety.

The Eastern band of Shoshonis of Green and Wind River has been referred to as Chief Washakie's Band. Washakie was a spokesperson for the Shoshoni people. He led his Eastern band through prowess and valor.

Chief Washakie led the Shoshoni band for 60 years. When the Chief was nearing 70, he overheard members of the council talking about replacing him and said he was too old to be a war-chief.

The old Chief mounted his horse and rode out of camp. No one heard from Washakie for two months. They thought that he had died in reclusion. Washakie proved he was not too old to be chief.

One day the proud Washakie rode into camp. Six enemy scalps hung from his belt. That evening, a council meeting was held to determine who would be chief. Any successor would have to achieve greater deeds in order to replace Washakie as chieftain.

Fort Washakie was established as an Army post called Camp Augur after General Christopher Augur, Commander of the Platte. The post was renamed Camp Brown in honor of Captain Fredrick H. Brown killed in the Fetterman Massacre of 1866. Fort Fetterman was

Kit Carson, friend of
Chief Washakie
Photo Courtesy of Wikipedia

Chief Washakie's Son-in-Law
Jim Bridger, Mountain Man
Photo Courtesy of Wikipedia

later renamed Fort Washakie in 1878 to honor Chief Washakie. Fort Washakie was the only U.S. military outpost ever to be named for a Native American. Many features in Wyoming are named after the Chief, including a county, a small town, an historic center, a hot springs, and a fort.

Chief Washakie is revered as the most important chief of the Shoshoni tribe. The Shoshoni people honor Washakie today as do white people. Wyoming lists Washakie as one of the most important people in their history.

Eastern Shoshoni Chief Washakie was a friend to the United States, a statesman and diplomat to Washington D.C., a peace chief, who served as interpreter, mediator and scout for the U.S. Army. He was a popular Indian in the newspapers and the public. A statute of Chief Washakie stands in Casper, Wyoming.

Chief Washakie fought with and aided the U.S. Military against the Arapaho, Cheyenne, Sioux and Ute Indians and granted the United States the right-of-way for the Union Pacific Railroad. Chief Washakie received a silver saddle from President Ulysses S. Grant and a peace medal from President Johnson.

The famed Chieftain Washakie died on February 20, 1900 and was buried with full military honors like no other ceremony ever held for any American Indian. He was a devout Christian and a member of the Episcopal church. The graves of Sacajawea and Washakie are situated on the grounds of the Wind River Indian Reservation in the Wind River Mountains of Wyoming. Fort Washakie was an active military outpost until 1909, when it was decommissioned and given over to the Shoshoni Indian Agency.

Oxen Drawn Wagons on the Oregon Trail
Photo Courtesy of Wikipedia.org

CHAPTER TEN
WAGONS WEST

The missionaries, Marcus and Narcissa Whitman and Henry and Eliza Spalding had traveled overland by Conestoga wagon from New York, reaching Fort Boise, in 1836. Their wagon broke down on the trail, but was the first wagon to cross the plains. The useless remnant was abandoned at the Fort Boise. Hudson's Bay employees transported them from the fort west into Oregon Territory.

In 1841 Colonel John Bartleson and John Bidwell led an emigrant party wagon-train from St. Louis heading to Fort Hall, southwest through Snake Country along the Humboldt River, through what is now Nevada, over the mountains into California. They related the strangest tales about a party of curious Snake Indians who followed them for some time, but did not attack them.

Sarah Winnemucca, the chief's granddaughter, told a humorous tale of her grandfather going out to meet the first white men that the Paiute Indians had ever seen in his territory in present day Nevada. Indians came to old Chief Winnemucca and told him of white men with beards that made camp in their vicinity.

Winnemucca was happy and spoke, "My white brothers, my long looked-for white brothers have come at last!" The chief took his sub-chiefs and rode out to their camp, to greet them with open arms.

When the party of Paiutes arrived the teamsters were fearful and stopped them. There was no interpreter, so they used hand motions. Winnemucca acted out and threw down his robes proving that he was unarmed and meant no harm. Still, the white men halted their advance. Winnemucca was disappointed they did not greet him.

Each night as they camped, the Paiute stayed near them, escorting the party for several days. The chief had been so anxious to meet them. Finally, Winnemucca turned his party around and the Indians returned to their lodges. As the wagons rolled out of sight the emigrants thought they had escaped with their lives. Winnemucca returned home, saddened by the whole affair. This most likely was the Bartleson & Bidwell emigrant party, described earlier.

Later on, when Lieutenant John Fremont met the chief, it became a comedy of errors. Lieutenant Freemont asked "Old Winnemucca" a question. He would answer, "truckee, truckee," which in the Paiute language meant, "all right." Freemont assumed that his name was Truckee and recorded it that way. It stuck and Winnemucca became known as Chief Truckee. Chief Winnemucca scouted for Freemont during the Mexican War.

The old chief was now nicknamed, "Captain Truckee." Captain Truckee later accompanied a party of white men traveling over the mountains to California Territory in 1844.

The white man appeared on the scene at the turn of the 19th century. Fur traders came building forts. In 1842, wagon trains moved westward. Marcus Whitman headed up a massive wagon train into Oregon in 1843 along the Oregon Trail across Indian lands; thousands followed. The wagon trains rolled in a never ending stream.

Conflict arose among the settlers, who crossed Indian lands in covered wagons bound for Oregon and California. The emigrants killed game on Shoshoni hunting grounds. Settlers competed with the Indians for game, grassland and water on their own lands. White settlers drained Indian water holes for their livestock. Their cattle grazed plants and grasses down to the roots. Seeds that the Shoshoni gathered for food were destroyed. Thousands of emigrants crossed Shoshoni lands. Fighting occurred from Bear Valley to the Snake.

After 1843, emigrants embarked in vast numbers on the long 2,000 mile journey west from St. Louis along the Oregon Trail to their destinations in California and Oregon Territories. Women and children rode in wagons; others rode horses, mules or simply walked.

Shoshoni looked at foreigners that encroached on their land as invaders. Skirmishes and massacres occurred. Indians on the warpath attacked various settlers and massacred wagon trains.

Emigrant wagon trains dotted the horizon for miles. A number of wagons joined together to form one wagon train with safety in numbers. Guides were employed as train captains to lead the wagon trains. A vote sometimes determined who were the train captain and other officers. At night, wagons were formed in a circle (corral). Guards were posted for security. Many wagons went west.

Covered wagons, called ox-trains, were a common site on the Oregon Trail. A mule train was just as it sounds. Draft animals: horses, mules and oxen pulled wagons, but horses were costly.

Oxen sold for less, pulled more weight, were stationery at night, and their meat more edible. An oxen-pulled covered wagon covered 20 miles, daily. Two oxen pulled a Prairie-Schooner with two yokes. Freighters employed four oxen. Heat exhaustion killed mules and oxen on the trail and buzzards ate the carcasses picking them clean.

The pioneers faced hardship and danger on their trek west. Bandits, disease, extreme temperatures, flooded river crossings,

Indians, rattlesnakes, rough terrain, and wild animals faced them on their journey. Swarms of mosquitoes could plague the animals and humans in swamp land. Thousands of pioneers died on the trail.

Roads back then were crude over rough terrain. In the beginning roads were non-existent and had to be forged. Others began as migratory animal paths that became Indian hunting trails. Wagons blazed trails leaving ruts still seen today along the old Oregon Trail.

Many wagons were left abandoned and pieces of furniture were removed to lighten the emigrant's load. To see furniture littering the Oregon Trail became a familiar sight for those traveling west.

The Three Island Crossing was a very famous site to cross the Snake River and a major junction of the Oregon Trail that employed a ferry, yet one of the most treacherous river crossings. Besides being a major river crossing, the water there was potable.

Water, grass and firewood were available. Glenn's Ferry, a small town nearby was named for Gus Glenn, owner and operator of the river ferry. Glenn ferried hundreds of wagons across the River.

Thousands of pioneers passed this way. Some emigrants waited until late August to cross the Snake River after the water level had receded and forded the river across the gravel sandbars and followed the northern route.

Some of the wagons continued along the south side of the Snake River, the southern route of the Oregon Trail, but it was a more rugged trip.

There were two types of covered wagons: the Conestoga wagon was manufactured first and had broader wheels than the Prairie Schooner. The Conestoga wagon but was more cumbersome.

The Prairie Schooner weighed just one ton and outlived the Conestoga. They were compared to sailing ships on the ocean.

In 1848 the Columbia District became Oregon Territory, with Idaho, Oregon, Washington, Montana and Wyoming, west of the Continental Divide.

The first treaty between the Arapaho, Cheyenne, Crow, and Sioux and the United States was signed at Fort Laramie in 1851 and assigned boundaries to the tribes. Jim Bridger served as an interpreter with Washakie, his father-in-law. The Shoshoni did not sign, but attended, witnessed and agreed to tribal peace.

The Pony express ran from St. Louis to Sacramento. Riders carried mail, from 1860-1861. About the same time, stage-lines were established that were run mostly by independents. Stage-coaches carried freight, mail, passengers and payroll across western America.

A never ending line of settlers in wagons continued across Indian Territory. Immigrants killed the game. Their oxen, mules and horses ate the grassland and left little for their horses. They sat in their wagon seats and shot Indians as they passed.

Indians had their fill and were provoked to attack the wagon trains that rolled across their land. The slow moving processions were easy targets for Indians, who lay in ambush. They attacked the Perry train on August 19, 1854 as they crossed the Camas Prairie.

In August 1854, a wagon train moved slowly westward along the Boise River on the Oregon Trail; their next stop was Fort Boise on the Snake River. The Ward wagons of 23 people left the train, electing to have a picnic on the Boise and unhitched their wagons just south of Middleton, Idaho.

Older brother, Robert Ward ran into camp. He shouted, "The Indians have stolen a horse," and all hell erupted. Hitching up their horses, the Ward party pulled their rigs up onto the road, trying to escape, but were immediately surrounded by 200 Snake Indians.

The Indians approached and pretended to be trading horses; then, a shot rang out. Wagon-master, Alexander Ward, fell from his wagon, mortally wounded. Arrows and bullets flew. By sunset, all of the adult males in the party were murdered.

The warriors overpowered the remaining women and children in the party that had lived. Mrs. Ward, her teen-age daughter and two little girls were tortured and killed.

Three children simply vanished. Indians took white women and children captive for slaves or brides, burned the wagons and fled. During the attack the teen-age Ward boys, both struck by arrows, crawled into the brush and escaped.

A very brave William had walked 25 miles to Fort Boise, with an arrow through his lung. Newton was later found alive! It became known that British traders at Fort Boise had sold guns, ammo, and whiskey to the Indians that could have incited the massacre.

Snake Indians were blamed for the bloodshed. At Fort Dalles, Major Rains ordered Haller and 26 soldiers to pursue them. They rode ahead of the Nez Perce and Umatilla scouts.

Special Agent Olney concluded that there were approximately 3,000 Snake Indians on the Snake River Plain of which he was Superintendent. The eastern Idaho and the western Wyoming Shoshonis were under the Utah Indian Affairs Jurisdiction.

At the massacre site, Haller buried 18 bodies and picked up the renegade Indians' trail into the mountains, but stopped the search for the time as winter approached.

They caught and lynched 18 Indians responsible for the attacks; the exact number killed in the massacre. They had killed 18 settlers, stole their livestock and burned their wagons. The Ward Massacre Memorial on the old Oregon Trail is a monument to them.

Indians just followed behind wagon trains. Settlers could not tell if they were peaceful or warlike. 1860-1863, Snakes made a series of raids in eastern Idaho. On October 16, 1860, Indians massacred the Utter Party, west of Castle Butte in early Owyhee County. August 9, 1862, the Smart wagon train traveled west followed by the Adams, Wilson and Kennedy trains. One half mile from Massacre Rocks, a Snake war-party ambushed and killed the Smart family.

Chiefs Snag, Tendoy and Washakie caused little problems and were peaceable, but Chiefs Bear Hunter and Pocatello were on the rampage attacking wagon trains crossing their country in 1859. It was later determined that Chief Pocatello of the Bear River Shoshoni was responsible for the preceding massacres.

Eighteen year old Starr Wilkinson was the 6 foot 8 inch, 300 pound half-breed son of a Cherokee Indian-negro mother and a white father. He started west in 1856, from St. Louis by wagon-train. Starr loved a girl, named Jesse Smith, who jilted him for a Mr. York.

Wilkinson caught the two lying in the sagebrush, on the Snake River. He wrestled with the man, drowned him in the river and later jumped the train. He met a party of Paiute Indians and joined their band. They called him "Nampa," in Paiute or "Bigfoot." He led them and teamed up with Joe Lewis, a notorious French Canadian.

The wagon-train returned to St. Louis, due to harsh winter; when they returned, Nampa and his Paiute band massacred them and burned the wagons. He led the renegades on stagecoach raids along Reynolds Creek on the Boise-Silver City road. Nampa (who never rode a horse) ran along-side a moving stage giving off war-whoops scaring the passengers to death. The outlaws became a nuisance.

The Army found a 17 1/2" bare footprint on the Weiser River. The story of "Bigfoot" appeared in the Idaho Statesman in 1868 and offered of a $1,000.00 reward for "BIGFOOT," DEAD or ALIVE.

When Bigfoot ran along-side the stagecoach again, bounty hunter John Wheeler waited in the Aspen trees with his 44 caliber repeating long-rifle. He shot Bigfoot, who vanished. Wheeler saw a tumble-weed moving along the ground. He began firing at the weed.

The hulk of a man began running wildly in Wheeler's direction. He shot Bigfoot 16 times. Wheeler apologized for shooting him to disable the last limb. Nampa related his life story in exchange for an Indian burial and died at 30 years of age. Chief Nampa became the namesake of the town of "Nampa, Idaho." The "Bigfoot" legend didn't end and rumors of Bigfoot or his ghost are yet alive in the Owyhee desert and the Northwest, today.

The Boise River and Camas Prairie chiefs Amaroko (Buffalo-Meat-Behind-the-Shoulder) and Pocmacheah (Hairy Man) were sub-chiefs under Bannock Chief Pasigo (Sego Lily). Chief Pasigo was blamed for the Fort Lemhi massacre.

134

Sioux Chief Sitting Bull
Photo Courtesy of Wikimedia.org

General George Armstrong Custer
Photo Courtesy of Wikipedia.org

CHAPTER ELEVEN
INDIAN WARS

The Seminole Wars were fought in 1817-1818. The Seminole Indians lost. Jackson negotiated nine out of ten peace treaties in the east. Indians east of the Mississippi were conquered by the U.S. Army, forced to relinquish millions of acres of land to the United States and were pushed off their land. Settlers had pressured the government to acquire Indian lands for them to plant crops and build homes. The Indian Removal Act was signed into law May 28, 1830, by President Jackson. It authorized him to grant unsettled lands west of the Mississippi for Indian lands within eastern state borders.

In 1834, a region of Oklahoma was established as "Indian Territory," a former possession of the United States Indian Territory covered 31,000 square miles. Indians were displaced east of the Mississippi to "Indian Territory," which included Kansas, Nebraska and Oklahoma Territories and later was reduced to Oklahoma.

Creek, Cherokee, Chickasaw, Delaware, and Seminole Indian tribes were honored as "the Five Civilized Tribes." In the fall of 1838-39, the Cherokee Indians had to trek on a forced march cross country on the "Trail of Tears" to Indian Territory in Oklahoma; 4,000 Cherokees died on the long journey. It was an impossible trek.

Comanche fought the palefaces during the Texas-Indian Wars, since 1840. Comanche and Southern Plains Indians resisted the palefaces' advance for years and fought the Texas Rangers. Indians were hesitant to possess assigned lands, due to Comanche war parties.

Some emigrants were so paranoid of Indians that they shot them on sight. This caused the Paiutes to fear the pioneers traveling west. During the great "California Gold Rush of 1849," miners began encroaching on Paiute lands. When Silver was discovered in Nevada Territory the Paiute woes increased. Prospectors in Silver City, Gold City, and Virginia City all had silver-strikes.

Thousands of miners moved into the area and cut the Paiute's pinion pines for mine shacks. Mules grazed on plants, grasses and seeds normally eaten by the Indians. Cyanide from silver mines leaked into their streams, killing the fish. White man drove off the game; miners stole Paiute's horses. Indians stole livestock as revenge.

In 1843, wagon trains began moving westward along the Oregon Trail by the hundreds. Indians went on the warpath attacking settlers and massacring them. Hundreds of pioneers passed through the Whitman Mission bringing disease that affected Indians. Cayuse Indians dropped like flies. Whitman had warned them, but they bathed in cold water to combat the high fever and died as a result. Angered by the epidemic, the stricken Indians knew the measles came from the Mission. In 1847, the Cayuse went on the war path.

The sick were being attended at the Whitman Mission on November 29, 1847. Without warning, a Cayuse War-Party ambushed Rev. and Mrs. Whitman and massacred eleven others; they left two girls to die. Dozens of women and children were taken hostage. Thirteen people escaped into the woods and made it to Fort Vancouver or reached Lapwai Mission. The Cayuse War had begun.

During the massacre, Nez Perce took Mrs. Spalding and her children to a safe-house, home of Indian Agent, William Craig, the first white settler in Idaho. They respected Craig, who married a Nez Perce. He left his horse and fled with the help of Nez Perce women.

When the survivors reached Fort Vancouver, chief factor McLoughlin sent Peter Skene Ogden to represent the Hudson's Bay Company. Ogden traded 50 blankets, 50 shirts, handkerchiefs, tobacco, guns and ammunition for the captives' lives. He brought 37 captives back to Fort Vancouver in 1848. Five leaders of the massacre were caught in October, 1849, tried and hanged in Oregon City in 1850. The Cayuse War ended and the missions were closed down.

In 1851, the Treaty at Fort Laramie was signed by the Arapaho, Cheyenne, Crow, and Sioux tribes. Sioux Chiefs Spotted Tail, Roman Nose, Old-Man-Afraid-of-His-Horses, Lone Horn, Whistling Elk, Pipe and Slow Bull met with agents to negotiate peace.

In 1854, a Sioux Indian killed a Mormon's ox at Fort Laramie. Lt. Grattan led his troops into a Sioux village near the Platte River demanding vengeance. The Sioux killed Grattan and all his troops. In 1854, the Ward Wagon train was massacred by a band of renegade Shoshoni Indians. The Modoc Indians rebelled in 1855.

The Snake country massacres began as the Snake Indians attacked wagon trains, Army units and supply trains from 1854-1859. The Snakes were on the rampage from Utah into Oregon country.

It was dangerous to be at Fort Boise or Fort Hall. Indian trouble closed both forts in 1856. The Army fought the Yakima Indians in 1856. The Palouse Indians, in northern Idaho, executed raids in 1858 and stole emigrants' cattle. Major Steptoe led a military fight against the Coeur d'Alene, Palouse and Spokane in 1858.

In 1859, two miners were killed by Indians, causing the Yakima Indian War. The Army defeated them and confined them to the reservation. Army escorts were then provided for wagon trains.

Poito was born in 1820 to Shoshoni parents in Oregon Territory. He married the daughter of Old Chief Winnemucca and was inducted into the Paiute tribe in Paiute tribal custom. Poito was given the name of Winnemucca. He was also called, "Bad Face." He became chief of the Kuyuidika band of the Northern Paiutes and influenced the Carson, Humboldt and Walker River Paiutes. Winnemucca II was less trusting of the white man than his father-in-law, Chief Truckee. Yet, he tried to keep the peace.

Two Paiute maidens digging roots were kidnapped. Natchez Winnemucca (Sarah's brother) and other Paiutes scoured the countryside. They rescued the two girls that were bound and gagged in a cellar outside of Carson City, causing a Paiute uprising. A Northern Paiute council was called at Pyramid Lake; while they were in council two white men were killed at William's Station. They decided on war; Chief Winnemucca was a proponent.

The Pyramid Lake War of 1860 was provoked by a dishonest Indian Agent, who held back food, money and seed from the Paiutes at Fort McDermott and Pyramid Lake. The kidnapping incident was the last straw. Winnemucca's band could not take it any longer. The chief declared war. The Paiute War of 1860 ensued.

Army Major Ormsby and about 100 men searched for the Paiute band in order to punish them, following their tracks along the Truckee River for about 100 miles. On May 13, 1860, the Paiute War between Northern Paiutes, some Bannock and Shoshoni and the white settlers was fought in a meadow near Pyramid Lake (now Nevada).

Chief Winnemucca formed his 600 warriors in a semi-circle on a low hill. The fighting escalated. Natchez Winnemucca saw that

Paiute Warrior, Paiute War of 1860
(Courtesy of Wikimedia.org)

Major Ormsby was in trouble and rode to help his friend, but it was too late. A brave rode in and shot him before the Major could be reached. Seventy settlers and 25 Paiutes were killed. Sorties followed. Peace was reached in August with no treaty. After the battle, U.S. soldiers were dispatched from California that outnumbered the Paiutes, who retreated into the mountains joining their families.

Fort Churchill was established in 1860 in order to protect the Pony Express Riders and settlers. Land was designated for a reserve at Pyramid Lake. Col. Lander set up a meeting with Winnemucca.

In the 1860's, about the same time of the Paiute War in the Nevada Territory, Northern Paiute Chief Paulina and his band were on the rampage in central Oregon Territory. Chief Paulina was on the war trail; he attacked the settlers, stole horses and livestock as well as assaulting Indian reservations, resulting in many deaths.

United States President Abraham Lincoln ordered the U.S. Army to the western front to protect the emigrant wagon trains, miners and settlers from Indian attacks and to contain the Indians. Skirmishes ensued in Idaho and the surrounding territories between the Indians and whites and the U.S. Cavalry was called in to fight.

Major Lugenbeel established Camp River Boise, in 1863 at the time of the Civil War, an outpost used to fight Indians. Both Boise City and Camp River Boise (Fort Boise) evolved at the same time. Fort Boise was an extension of Fort Vancouver. As the Civil War wound down, Indian fighters arrived.

A U.S. Cavalry pony soldier was issued a horse, saddle, dark blue tunics, light blue trousers, belt, socks, boots, neckerchief, cap and jacket. Weapons issued were a 45 caliber rifle, 45 caliber pistol, ammo and saber. A soldier's life was hard back then; he spent hours in the saddle, lacked sleep, and was exposed to sun, wind, and rain. Winters were grueling in the mud, ice and snow in the line of duty.

George Washington originated the peace medal that bore his image and gave medals to peaceable Indian chiefs. The first twenty U.S. Presidents in succession issued them. The Bluecoats had duties besides combat. They wrote treaties with the Indians and smoked the peace pipe with them. They gave peace medals to the Indian chiefs.

Miner's struck gold in 1862 in the Boise Basin in Idaho City, Silver City, Coeur d'Alene and Salmon River. Miners found gold on the Nez Perce Reservation, and opened mining whereas thousands of miners migrated to Idaho Territory. Lewiston's Tent City was named the capital of Idaho Territory.

Idaho City was a boom town with the largest population in the northwest. Prospectors led by George Grimes left Oregon Territory for the Boise Basin, in July of 1862 with some Bannock Indians as guides; six miles outside Bannock (present day Idaho City) they found gold, but the Bannocks ambushed them, killing Grimes.

The Indian Wars were followed by the Great Sioux Wars. The Snake River War (1864-1868) followed and was fought between the U.S. Army and the Bannock, Paiute and Shoshoni "Snakes." Fighting extended across California, Idaho, Nevada and Oregon.

In 1865, the Black Hawk War was waged between the Ute, Paiute and Navajo Indians, led by Chief Black Hawk. The Texas-Indian Wars coincided with the Utah Black Hawk War.

April 1866, Cheyenne Chief Dull Knife and Sioux Chiefs Red Cloud and Spotted Tail met with other chiefs at Fort Laramie to discuss use of Powder River country. Col. Henry Carrington and 700 infantrymen rode into the fort ready to build forts in Sioux territory. Red Cloud left the peace table in June of 1866, ready for war.

Autumn of 1866, Red Cloud returned to the Powder River country; his scouts reported *"wasichus,"* (palefaces) had advanced 200 miles from Fort Laramie into Sioux territory on the Bozeman Trail. He summoned scattered bands of Arapaho, Cheyenne, and Sioux to assemble after their bison hunts. Red Cloud declared war on America, after the U.S. Army built forts on Sioux hunting grounds.

Red Cloud became angry and spoke, *"The Great Father sends us presents and wants us to sell him the road, but the white chief goes with soldiers to steal the road before the Indians could say yes or no."* The angry chief prophesied of Carrington and his troops in their land, *"In two moons, the command will not have a hoof left."*

Chief Crazy Horse led a Sioux war party on a raid against Horseshoe Station March 19, 1868. Fetterman's Outpost and Elliot's Squadron, on the Wichita were wiped out in 1868 by the Comanche.

Sherman ordered his officers to destroy all Sioux camps to reduce their numbers. Red Cloud's prediction came true despite the Army's efforts. Red Cloud closed the Bozeman's Trail and all three forts. He was a great Sioux leader who fought the western expansion of whites until 1868, successful in defeating the U.S. Army in battle. Sioux chiefs remained unwilling to sell the Black Hills.

Red Cloud came to Fort Laramie ending the Powder River War and signed "The Treaty of Laramie," November 6, 1868. He relinquished the Black Hills, received the perimeters for the Great Sioux Reservation at Rosebud and kept their hunting grounds.

General Nelson A. Miles
In 1895, Nelson A. Miles was promoted to the rank of Army General
as Commander and Chief of the U.S. Army.
Photo Courtesy of Wikimedia.org

The Treaty of Medicine Lodge was signed between the U.S. Army and the Comanche, Cheyenne and the Plains Apache Indians in 1867. The Bannock met in council with the U.S. Army at Long Creek in 1867. The Army counseled with the Bannock and convinced them to go onto the reservation.

Hoping to keep their old way of life, Bannock Chief Tahgee insisted on retaining the Camas Prairie an important part of maintaining their subsistence as part of the reservation and to be able to continue to hunt buffalo. The Army recorded his request, but wrote down "Kansas Prairie," instead.

On July 3, 1868, Chief Tahgee and nearly 800 Bannocks and hundreds of Shoshoni met at Bridger to sign the treaty for a reservation. The Bannock word was good; they had kept the peace between the 1863 and the 1868 Treaties and were friendly to settlers.

The Fort Bridger Treaty made division between the Goshiute (Eastern) Shoshoni (Utah) and the *Wihinasht* (Western Shoshoni) the Boise, Bruneau and Weiser Shoshoni. The Salmon-eater and Sheep-eater Shoshoni were referred to as the Northern Shoshoni Indians. The Western and Northern Shoshoni all lodged in Idaho Territory.

The treaty made revision for a Shoshoni Bannock Indian reservation. The Fort Bridger Treaty of 1868 was signed by President Andrew Johnson of the United States of America and the Eastern Shoshoni and Bannock of the Territory of Utah. General W.T. Sherman and other U.S. Army officers signed the treaty.

Bannock Indians that signed were the 1868 Treaty of Fort Bridger were Tahgee, Taytoba, Wertzewonagen, Cooshagan, Pansookamotse, and Awiteetse. Shoshoni Indians that signed were

Washakie, Waunypitz, Toopsepowot, Narkok, Taboonshe, Bazeel, Pantoshega and Ninnybitse. Each made his mark to sign.

In 1868, the Sioux Indians drove the Bannock and Shoshoni tribes out of Yellowstone. In August of 1868, both the Bannock and Shoshoni Indians were camped long the Boise River. They were allowed to hunt the buffalo come autumn. In 1869, the Sioux Indians went on the war path and killed 29 Bannock and Shoshoni Indians.

The Bannock hunted buffalo with the Eastern Shoshoni in the Wind River Mountains. On route home, they stopped at Fort Hall in order to receive their presents. While they were there, Chief Tahgee told the Indian Agent that they were ready to move to Fort Hall. Before the Lemhi left the reservation for Fort Hall Tendoy, the last Lemhi Chief and his sub-chiefs made their marks to ratify the removal agreement, but two-thirds of the bands' signatures were lost. The government has not produced them for the last 25 years.

On the twenty third of April, 1869, Agent Powell led 850 Bruneau Shoshoni, 300 Boise Shoshoni and 150 Bannock Indians from Boise to the Fort Hall Reservation. On July 30, 1869, President Grant gave the executive order to grant the Bannock Indians a home at Fort Hall Indian Reservation in Idaho. The Governor was informed of the decision and word was passed on to the Indian Commissioner.

The U.S. Army moved other Indians onto reservations by 1870, confiscated their guns and shot their horses to limit their movement. Hostiles were relocated onto government reservations.

The Indian Appropriation Act was passed which removed government recognition of tribes as independent political entities. For 200 years, horses revolutionized the Amerindians' world. The horse and Indian era was a good one. Indians loved their horses, but the romance between the horse and Indian was short lived.

In 1871, the U.S. government sponsored the wholesale slaughter of bison herds to force the Plains Indians onto reservations. Bison were needlessly slaughtered by the thousands. The Indians had lived luxuriously on the buffalo for centuries, but the government removed the bison and caused much sacrifice and starvation. It was about this time that the Indians began to go out in war parties in order to steal horses and livestock from the settlers to provide food.

In 1873, Isatai, a Comanche Shaman, prophesied that the buffalo would return if they killed the white intruders. Arapaho, Comanche, Kiowa and Cheyenne attacked the U.S. Cavalry on the Southern Plains during the Red River War of 1874.

Beaten, Chief Quanah Parker and 400 warriors entered Fort Sill driving 1500 head of horses, surrendered June 2, 1875 and agreed to stay. The Army confiscated their guns and shot their horses to hold them. The last of the combatants were relocated to reserves. Peace had not come easy. Indian Agents gave the Indians seeds to plant.

The Sioux were ordered to the Rosebud reservation. If they had refused, the Sioux would have been considered hostiles or non-reservation Indians. The war on the Sioux began on February 1,1876. General Crook embarked from Fort Walla-Walla. His intent was to move through the Powder River Valley to spearhead the attack against the Sioux. The battle at Powder River was a wash. March 1876, Crook moved his troops back to Fort Fetterman and quartered for the winter.

On June 14, 1876, Crook was joined by Chiefs, Good Heart, Medicine Crow, Old Crow and 176 Crow scouts. Washakie and 86 Shoshoni warriors arrived to fight the warring Sioux, who killed his son. They rode in eloquently and joined the ranks.

After a 60 mile ride from Wind River, the Shoshoni did a war dance into the night wearing war paint and war bonnets. They danced through the night to the beat of the tom-toms. The soldiers were kept awake all night listening to the chants, war-whoops and drums and watched the Indians dance into the wee hours of the morning.

General Crook broke camp, crossed the Tongue River and turned northwest into Sioux territory. Indian scouts rode out ahead of the troops and reported seeing Sioux hunting buffalo and found their tracks indicating movement of many Sioux.

Finding an Indian trail, Crook deployed Reynolds and six men to scout for the village. He marched through snow and cold surprising the Cheyenne and Sioux and seized the village, but Reynolds returned to the fort and did not destroy the lodges.

General Crook's troops bivouacked at the headwaters of Rosebud Creek. At dawn, they marched downstream. Crook commanded a halt around 8:00 a.m.; they grazed their horses. His infantry caught up.

The Crow-Shoshoni scouts regrouped and met the second Sioux assault on the Great Sioux Reservation. They advanced to a hilly arena that rose to higher elevations. The Crow grew uneasy unprepared for a sudden Sioux attack. Medicine Crow and Washakie sent out look-outs on elevated ridges. Others searched for tracks.

149

His Indian scouts called Crook, "Three Stars," the number of stars on his uniform; he was the Army's greatest Indian fighter. Crook treated Indians humanely and negotiated instead of fighting. Sioux hunters returned to their village to report seeing Crook's camp.

Suddenly, a wounded warrior rode in at a full gallop, shouting, "Sioux, Sioux, many Sioux." Shots were fired as Crook's scouts counter attacked 500 yards ahead. They attacked from the north and west issuing war whoops as the advance party held the Sioux back.

On June 17th, Brigadier General Crook attacked the Sioux near the headwaters of the Rosebud. Crook's "long-knives" fought the hostiles and were pushed back by Chief Crazy Horse's Cheyenne and Sioux Indian warriors at the Battle of Rosebud River.

The next day Crook retreated to the south. As he withdrew, 7,000 Sioux moved their village to the east bank of the Little Bighorn River to hunt buffalo. About 2,000 of the Sioux people were warriors.

Chief Crazy Horse held his massive army back in reserve. It was estimated that there were 2,500 Arapahoe, Cheyenne, and Sioux all hidden in the hills. Perhaps 1,500 were in the initial charge.

Crook backed his Indian scouts and deployed more in the valley. Washakie spoke to Crook as he rode alongside him, using sign language to discuss the battle.

He urged his sub-chiefs into battle. Chief Washakie helped rescue an injured officer. The Chief fought naked to the waist; he sat on his war pony in deerskin britches and moccasins with a long war bonnet that hung down to the ground. Washakie and his Shoshoni band had always been friendly to the white man. Now, he had brought his army to help fight the Sioux enemy.

Sioux War Chiefs
Photo Courtesy of Legends of America.com

Crow-Shoshoni scouts regrouped and met the second Sioux assault head on. Some dismounted and fought from the ground. Others rode bravely among the Sioux and fought at close range. The advance guard of Indian scouts saved Crook's column from certain death. He counted his loses, on Rosebud Creek and chose to retreat.

The Laramie Treaty divided the Teton Sioux into two groups: reservation Indians and hostile (non-treaty) Indians that dwelled in the Powder River country led by Chief Sitting Bull, a Hunkpapa Sioux medicine man.   He had a dream and envisioned soldiers that descended on them like grasshoppers, but fell to the ground in defeat.

An overconfident George Armstrong Custer led his cavalry all night in order to reach Rosebud Sioux Indian Village in South Dakota Territory.   Custer excited about fighting the Sioux had refused to believe that he was headed for disaster and was eager to massacre the Indians. He did not take the advice of his Crow scouts to retreat because of the Sioux's numbers. Custer was outnumbered, surrounded by the Sioux war party. Two hundred ten men were massacred by Sioux warriors in the Battle of the Little Bighorn.

War-Chiefs Gall and Crazy Horse and their Sioux warriors were credited with conquering the 7th Cavalry in the Battle of the Little Bighorn. Custer died that day on June 25, 1876.

Captain Nelson A. Miles was revered and arguably the most respected American soldier of his era.   He volunteered with the Army just after the start of the American Civil War. Plains Tribes surrendered to Capt. Miles in his 1876-77 campaign at Pine Ridge, South Dakota.   Sitting Bull and his Oglala Sioux had resisted. The Great Sioux Wars lasted from 1866-1876.

Nez Perce Chief Joseph's scouts observed the procession of soldiers coming to fight. Captain Perry's U. S. Cavalry, militia and scouts arrived in White Bird Canyon and at dawn June 17, 1877. Perry and two companies rode down the steep hill into the canyon.

About 300 yards out, troops led by Lt. Theller saw six Nez Perce on horseback carrying a white flag. Rifle fire broke the silence, and then another. Ad Chapman, Theller's scout, had fired two rounds that struck the dirt near the flag bearers.

The action started the Nez Perce War. The Nez Perce had no recourse, but to fight. Indian observers on horseback scattered on the field and returned fire.

It was a stand-off. Perry's men fired on the Indians and began the clash. The Nez Perce War of 1877 had begun. Joseph and 200 warriors with his whole village of men, women and children herding 2,000 horses moved from White Bird Hill across country in a running battle with the U.S. Army for hundreds of miles to Yellowstone northward into the Bear Paw Mountains in Montana.

General Miles intercepted Chief Joseph, demanded surrender, and assured safe passage. Cheyenne scouts spoke with Joseph and told him they believed Miles wanted peace. Joseph met with Miles. On the fifth day of talks, October 5, 1877, Chief Joseph surrendered, giving up his rifle. He uttered those famous words:

"Here me my chiefs, I am tired. My heart is sick and sad; from where the sun now stands, I will fight no more forever."

His flight to King George's land had failed. It is a little known fact that General Miles and Chief Joseph had remained good friends long after the war ended. He is referred to as a good Indian.

There was a lack of food on Fort Hall Indian Reservation. In 1878, the Indian Agent told the Indians that resided there that they should go out and hunt off the reservation. Bannock Chief Buffalo Horn visited the Territorial Governor and requested permission to purchase $2.00 worth of ammunition in order to hunt deer. Indians were free to hunt off reservation so the settlers spread rumors of Indian wars. Buffalo Horn rode to Camas Prairie and found that cattle men grazed cows and settlers let their pigs to root on the camas bulbs.

Chief Tendoy chose peace. Boise Shoshoni Captain Jim and Tendoy and his band rode to the Lemhi River Reservation. Because of broken treaties, Buffalo Horn declared war on the United States. On June 10, 1878, Buffalo Horn led his war party of 200 Bannock, Paiute and Weiser Indians on the war trail across Idaho Territory.

On the war path, Buffalo Horn's band of 200 Bannock Indians attacked cattlemen on the Camas Prairie and killed two of them; a third man hid in the brush, another found a horse and fled on horseback to Fort Boise where he contacted Captain Bernard, quartered there with his troops. Bernard led his troops and rode to Camas Prairie in pursuit of the renegades.

The marauders plundered wagons near King Hill, stole arms, and fled across the Snake River using the ferry. Reaching the other side, they cut it loose. The Bannocks killed some settlers at the mouth of the Bruneau River.

Captain Egan along with 46 Bannocks and Weiser Indians joined Buffalo Horn. His band increased to 300. Bernard's column pursued Buffalo Horn over the divide to the headwaters of the Owyhee River. Twenty volunteers, stationed at Silver City reached

War-chief Buffalo Horn Leader
of the Bannock War of 1878.
Photo Courtesy of the Idaho State
Historical Society Library

Sergeant Jim, Bannock Warrior
Courtesy of the Idaho
State Historical Society

the hostiles first and engaged them, meeting heavy fire. They retreated in a running battle; Chief Buffalo Horn was killed in the siege. Egan replaced him and their numbers grew to 800, as others joined them, outnumbering Bernard's men three to one. It was rumored that Buffalo Horn lived and escaped to Wyoming.

Howard left Fort Walla-Walla for Boise June 9, 1878. By June 18th, he had raised 900 troops, six officers and artillery to handle the outbreak. Captain Bernard and several other excellent officers joined General Howard's columns to engage Egan's band.

There is a folk story about a chief seen by trappers along the Humboldt River, wearing only one moccasin. Once, he came into town wearing little of nothing. The Old Chief Winnemucca was given an army uniform and hat, which he liked and wore.

During the Bannock War the warring Indians took old Chief Winnemucca II and the Malheur Paiutes at the reservation captive, taking their blankets, horses and weapons. When Sarah Winnemucca learned of her father's plight, she rode to Sheep Camp. She arrived desperate to find her father and met with U.S. Army General Howard, who gave her a letter of safe passage. Picking up the Bannock's tracks, Sarah rode after the Bannock raiders.

From a high overlook Sarah surveyed the Bannock camp of several hundred teepees. At nightfall she descended the slope. Sarah entered the chief's teepee under a blanket and war-paint. In the night, she ushered her father out of camp joined by her brother, his wife and two cousins. They held the horses and aided in the escape to Sheep Camp where the army escorted Sarah, her father and family to Fort McDermott and safety. Sarah worked for the army as a courier.

Nez Perce Chief Joseph the Patriotic Chief
General Miles and Chief Joseph became friends
their friendship that lasted a lifetime.
Photo Courtesy of Azusa Publishing, L.L.C.

Captain Egan rode toward the John Day River, in Oregon Territory. As they continued westward they killed ranchers and stole livestock along the Grand River.

The war party rode into the Blue Mountains. The hostiles were made up of Malheur, Paiute, Shoshoni, Umatilla, and Weiser Indians. The savages continued their rampage, killing and pillaging; on the move, they covered hundreds of miles.

The rebels fought whenever the Cavalry overtook them, who purposely kept the renegades on the run. The Army purposefully used those tactics in order to tire the Indians out. The Cavalry caught up with the escaping Bannocks in Oregon near Dead Man's Pass.

Egan (Pony Blanket) challenged Col. Robbins to a duel. They sat on their horses about 50 yards apart; Egan spurred his pony. They raced towards each other on horseback. Egan fired wildly under his horse's neck, Indian fashion. Robbins rode toward him, guns blazing. A bullet knocked Egan from his horse. He was left for dead.

But, Robbins had not killed him. Yet, Egan made a rapid recovery. Egan's mixed band crossed the Columbia River and offered the Umatilla Indians 2,000 horses to unite with them in battle.

When they refused, the rebels opened fire on them. The Umatilla Indians returned and pretended to join them, opened fire and killed Egan. Many died, the renegades scattered.

Some surviving Bannocks had crossed into Idaho Territory and attacked whites along the Salmon River and Payette Lake into Montana. Captain Miles, with 75 Cavalry troops plus Crow scouts managed a surprise attack on the Bannock in an early morning raid in the autumn of 1878, killing 11 ending the Bannock War.

Lemhi Chief Tendoy and Wife
(Photos Courtesy of Wikimedia.org)

Fort Hall Reservation Chief Tendoy
& George La Vatta, interpreter

Hostile Weiser Indians were being held in confinement at Fort Boise. Indians stole 14 horses in Indian Valley. A settler party rode to retrieve the ponies, but turned back at Cascade Falls.

Clusters of hostiles were seen camped at Yankee Fork and Cape Horn. Others withdrew to Salmon Country and joined Sheep-eater Indians. The agitated Indians were a constant menace to the miners. Sheep-eaters were accused of stealing cattle at Prairie Basin, in 1879.

Two prospectors died near Warren's Ranch. Five Chinese were killed by Loon Creek north east of Boise. Oro Grande was set ablaze and gutted. Howard feared all had joined forces.

Bannock, Blackfeet, Crow, and Nez Perce could hunt in Yellowstone for a time, but this right was later revoked along with their access to the park. Others were forced to give up their rights to the park and large portions of land and move to Fort Hall.

In 1880, the government banned the "Sun Dance" in order to force the Indians to accept the American culture. The Army had used ambush, disease, massacre, removal of the Indians from their lands, killing off the buffalo, reduction of land and warfare to defeat the natives and persuade them to move onto the reservations.

Those who chose war found themselves engaged with the Cavalry. Their fight was short lived. The U.S. Army engaged the Indians in combat. As one Indian War ended, another war began. The Indians fought but lost their fight. There was no choice but to surrender. They had fought a brave fight. They did all that they could to defend their homeland. Bows and arrows were no match for modern armies and weaponry.

Paiute Chief Winnemucca II
(Photo Courtesy of
Wikipedia.org)

Sarah Winnemucca of the
Northern Paiute Tribe
(Photo Courtesy of
Wikipedia.org)

Shoshoni Chiefs at Duck Valley
Photo Courtesy of Idaho State Historical Society Library

CHAPTER TWELVE
SHOSHONI RESERVATIONS

Treaties were written between the Army and the Bannock and Shoshoni Indians. The Soda Springs Treaty was written on October 14, 1863. All the treaties were un-ratified. The Wells Indian Village arose from the 1863 treaty. The Treaty of Fort Boise, October 10, 1864 was held. The Bruneau Treaty was written April 12, 1866. The Shoshoni made their marks at the Treaty of Long Tom Creek in 1867.

The Bannock and Eastern Shoshoni tribes signed the Treaty of Fort Bridger on July 3, 1868. The reservation was established by the Fort Bridger Treaty. The Bannock and Shoshoni were moved onto the Fort Hall reservation with a Military escort.

The Bannock and Shoshoni Indians were forced to forfeit their land to the U.S. government. Their children were taken from them and sent to white man's schools. Still, Indian hung on to their tradition and language the best that they could. Their old way of life was fleeting and they did not have much control of it.

The Treaty provided that the Bannock Indians be able to make a home at the reservation and still hunt buffalo. A large number of Bannock and Shoshoni Indians left the reservation and trekked to the Camas Prairie, where they harvested the camas plant for food and could hunt buffalo, yet the buffalo were disappearing from the Plains. The Indians were expected to transition from the hunting and gathering life way to one of agriculture and live like the palefaces, but it did not provide ample food. Many grew hungry.

The Shoshoni Indians at Fort Hall were given 1.8 million acres, by the Great White Father, President of the United States. The

163

Dawes Act reduced millions of acres of the Fort Hall Reserve to less than half. The Indian Reorganization Act reversed the Dawes Act and gave back the authority for the Indians to self govern.

Every head of family was given 320 acres. Indians over 18 received $100.00 worth of seeds to plant the first year and $25.00 per year for 3 years. Children 6-16 were to receive a compulsory education. A list of annuity goods was payable on September 1 for 30 years at Fort Bridger. A list of employees and a physician was provided. Treaties of reservation lands had to be voted on by a majority of the tribes. Gifts were to be given for the best farming operation the first three years. Fugitives were to be arrested. The Indian Agent would make his home on the reservation.

The reservation was set apart for 600 Bannock Indians and many more Shoshoni Indians that consented to remain there. Those tribes reside at Fort Hall now. The Shoshone-Bannock Fort Hall Indian Reservation is located in southeastern Idaho, eight miles north of Pocatello. The majority of the tribe lived on the Fort Hall reservation with self governing rights afforded under the Fort Bridger Treaty of 1868.

Preserving much of the old tradition, the Shoshoni Sun Dance is held annually at Fort Hall and the Wind River Reservation. The tribal members host annual powwows and have the sweat lodge ceremonies of old and pray for each other, families and the tribe.

Fort Hall Indian Reservation remains a thriving community today. The Reservation is very much alive and hundreds of Indians still reside at the Fort Hall Shoshone-Bannock Indian Reservation. There are businesses, a restaurant, schools and churches.

A seven member council was established in 1936, with a law and order code called the Fort Hall Business Council with 3500 Indians residing at Fort Hall, and 5,681 actual members called enrolled Indians. Non-members are called un-enrolled Indians.

A seven member council was established in 1936 and a Fort Hall Business Council. There are presently 3500 Indians residing at Fort Hall, with 5,000 actual members. The tribe has a tribal credit bureau, employment agency and recreation organization and manages its agriculture, commerce, casinos, credit bureau, employment agency, grocery, recreation, rural transits, schools and waste disposal.

In prehistoric times some tribes planted beans, corn and squash. Today, agriculture is the main income resource. The Indians farm 87,000 acres. Cattle and horses graze there. Sheep Creek and Mountain View Reservoirs provide fishing on the reservation. A third reservoir, the Billie Shaw, is being prepared. Shore birds and waterfowl flock to the wetland areas in great numbers. The public can camp, bird watch, fish or just relax and enjoy this recreation area.

During the winter of 1869, the Lemhi did not receive any appropriations. Chief Tendoy led 700 Indians of his band to Virginia City, Montana and made demands to the Governor of Montana for a reservation for his people on January 3, 1870.

Tendoy and four sub-chiefs met with Governor Ashley and three of his staff in his office. Under the agreement, signed by the chiefs, A.J. Smith, a long time friend of the Indians would represent them in Washington to secure settlement of the tribe on the Lemhi River. Tendoy asked for bullets to hunt buffalo in Montana in order to be able feed the Lemhi people.

On February 12, 1875, President Grant established the Lemhi Valley Indian Reservation for the exclusive use of the mixed tribes of the Bannock, Shoshoni, and Sheep-eater. The reserve was 100 square miles, for Sacajawea's people, on the Lemhi River, yet there were mixed feelings wanting a Military Fort in Lemhi Valley.

In 1907, 474 Snake Indians from mixed bands were banished and forcibly removed from their ancestral homelands. The Bannock, Sheep-eater and Lemhi Shoshoni Indians began the forced march from the Lemhi Reservation to Fort Hall, 400 miles to the south. They barely endured the trek that began 200 miles north of Fort Hall Indian Reservation in Idaho. This march was an extreme hardship for them and is referred to as "The Lemhi Trail of Tears." Many died along the way. Their reservation was abandoned in 1907.

Jealous of the Bannock's gifts, Sheep-eater Chief Tendoy and other Shoshonis remained on the Salmon. On May 1907, Chief Tendoy died and was buried at an Indian burial ground near Tendoy, Idaho.

The Lemhi Shoshoni's latest efforts are to restore federal recognition and return home to the Valley drainage area. The Agaideka (Salmon-Eater Shoshone) and Tukudeka (Sheep-eater Shoshone) who make up the Lemhi-Shoshone Tribes are considered the first residents of the upper Lemhi Valley.

The Duck Valley Indian Reservation was first established in 1877. The Shoshone-Paiute Reservation lies on the Idaho-Nevada border, half in each state, in Owyhee County, Idaho and Elko County, Nevada. In early times, the people occupied the reservation in earthen willow and sagebrush huts. The Indians struggled to survive.

166

The government failed to deliver their food and supplies. Some stayed because it was their people's ancestral home, but the government wanted the land for non-Indian homesteads.

Descendents of the Western Shoshoni and the Northern Paiute Indians occupy the Duck Valley Indian Reservation of Idaho-Nevada. On April 16, 1877 President Rutherford Hayes established the Western Shoshoni Indian Reservation.

During the Bannock War of 1878, some of the Northern Paiutes banded together with their Bannock kinsmen and were captured and sent to a prisoner of war camp in Yakima, Washington. Upon their release, the reservation was expanded to accommodate them. The bands survived the best that they could under the watchful eye of the Indian Agent and the Indian police.

In 1882, a physician was added. A small one room infirmary was built in 1897, which was replaced by a seven room infirmary in 1920. In 1937, a 20 bed infirmary was added with laboratory. In 1976 the infirmary was replaced by a modern Owyhee Community Health Facility.

In 1884, efforts were made to move the Western Shoshoni to Fort Hall, but the band headmen resisted. On May 4, 1886, Hayes expanded the reserve to include the Northern Paiute Indians. July 1, 1910, U.S. President William H. Taft expanded the reservation by another executive order.

A boarding school was in operation from 1884-1911. Three day schools were also operational. They closed in 1931 and the Swayne School was attended. High school students attended off reservation until 1946, when high school classes were added. In

1956, the reservation school system consolidated with the Elko, Nevada School District.

Tribal membership is over 2,000 with about 1700 living on the reservation. The Shoshoni-Paiute Tribe of Duck Valley still lodge on the original lands of their ancestors. The tribe has a business Council, a Chairman, Vice-Chairman and five Council Members managed by the Chairman all elected for 3 year terms. The Business Council conducts the Tribal government. There are four divisions of Tribal government: Health and Human Services, Judicial Services, Tribal Programs and Support Services.

The Duck Valley ranchers farm 12,000 acres of subjugated lands. The Shoshone-Paiute maintain 289,820 acres of land held in trust by the United States government for the use and occupancy of the Shoshoni-Paiute Indians and 22,231 acres of wetlands.

Wild Horse Reservoir was dug in 1936 for the Duck Valley Irrigation Project. Twelve hundred sixty five Native Americans were living on the Duck Valley Indian Reservation in the year 2,000.

The Wind River Reservation was established in 1868 for the Eastern Shoshoni shared with the Arapahoe Indians. The tribe of Chief Washakie, the Eastern Shoshoni, is located on the Wind River Reservation on 3,532,010 square miles in Fremont and Hot Springs Counties in west central Wyoming. The reserve occupies over two million acres with over 10,000 members.

Headquarters are at Fort Washakie. Wind River is home to the Northern Arapaho and the Eastern Shoshoni Indians. Each tribe has its own government. The Eastern Shoshoni number 2,650 Indians. There are 1,702 people in tribal headquarters. Sixty percent of the

Indians there have high school diplomas and six percent have at least Bachelor Degrees. There are four casinos on the reservation.

In 1960, the Lemhi Indians were disqualified to file a claim against the federal government for their ancestral lands. Instead, the suit was filed under the whole Shoshone-Bannock Tribe. They won their case and were awarded four and one half million dollars. The money was divided among 3,000 members on the Fort Hall Reservation, instead of the 500 Lemhi Shoshoni that resided there.

Ever since time began, man has been at war, mostly fighting to gain land. Reasons for war are enmity, politics and religion. Over the years, millions of people have been displaced because of wars. Immigrants came here for religious freedoms, but when they were in jeopardy from peril, the U.S. Army was called in to protect them from the American Indians and war was declared among them.

Western Shoshoni Indian Reserves have been established in Nevada, as follows: The Goshiute Reservation was established in 1914 at the Utah-Nevada border. Battle Mountain Reserve was begun in 1917. The Elko Reservation opened in 1918 and the Ely Colony in 1931. The Carlin Farm reservation was occupied from 1870-1879. The Death Valley Reservation was initiated at the turn of the century. The Yomba Reservation was initiated in 1937. The Duck Valley Reservation began in 1877 and the South Fork Reserve in 1941.

"Any man who thinks he can be happy and prosperous by letting the government take care of him had better take a closer look at the American Indian." Quote from Henry Ford, founder – Ford Motor Corporation

INDEX

172

Bibliography

Addison, Helen and McGrath, Dan L., *War Chief Joseph*, Lincoln, Nebraska, Third Bison Book Printing, 1967.

Barbour, Barton H., *Fort Union and the Upper Mississippi Fur Trade*, Norman, University of Oklahoma Press, 2001.

Beal, Merrill D., *"I Will Fight No More Forever,"* New York, Ballantine Books, 1971.

Bird, Laurie Annie, *Old Fort Boise*, Caldwell, Idaho, Caxton Printers, Ltd., 1971.

Brown, Dee, *Bury My Heart At Wounded Knee*, New York, Bantam, 1972.

Corless, Hank, *The Weiser Indians*, University of Utah Press, Salt Lake, 1990.

Dary, David, *The Oregon Trail, an American Saga*, New York, Oxford University Press, 2004.

Hailey, John, *History of Idaho*, Boise, Syms-York, 1910.

Kloss, Doris, *Sarah Winnemucca*, Minneapolis, Dillon Press, 1986.

Lowell, Helen & Peterson, Lucile, *Our First One Hundred Years*, Caldwell, Idaho, Caxton Printers, Ltd., 1999.

Members of the Potomac Corral, *Great Western Indian Fights*, Lincoln, Nebraska.,Bison Books, 1966.

Madsen, Brigham D., *The Bannock of Idaho*, Caxton Printers, Caldwell, Idaho, 1983

Madsen, Brigham D., *The Northern Shoshoni*, Caxton Printers, Caldwell, Idaho, 1980.

Madsen, Brigham D., *Chief Pocatello*, University of Idaho Press, Moscow, 1999.

O'Neal, Bill, *Best of the West*, Lincolnwood, Illinois, Publications International, Ltd., 2006.

Salisbury, Albert & Jane, *Lewis & Clark, the Journey West*, New York, Promontory Press, 1990.

Shannon, Donald H., *The Boise Massacre on the Oregon Trail*, Caldwell, Idaho, Snake River Publishers, 2004.

Steward, Julian H., *Plateau Aboriginal Sociopolitical Groups*, Salt Lake, University of Utah Press, 1970.

Utley, Robert M., *A Life Wild and Perilous, Henry Holt and Company, New York, 1997.*

Utley, Robert M., *Encyclopedia of the American West*, New York, Random House, 1997.

Welsh, James & Stekler, Paul, *Killing Custer*, New York, Norton and Company, 1994.

Wilson, Amy, *Comparative Analysis of Bead Assemblages* from the Fur Trade

Winnemucca, Sarah, *Life Among the Paiutes*, University of Nevada Press, Reno, 1994.

Posts Fort Colville and Fort Vancouver, /Thesis (M.S.)-University of Idaho, 1996, 180

Citing Electronic Publications

<http:www.tripcheck.com/poses/SBhellcanyon.asp>

<http:www.bigfootforums.com/lofiversion/index.php/tii5.68.html>

<http:www.blackhawkproductions.com/Walkara.htm>

<http:www.content.lib.utah.edu/utils.getlife/collection/USHSArchPub/id/76 89/filename/7724>

<http:www.clarkontheyellowstone.org/sig_event.html>

<http:www.enwikipedia.org/wiki/Washakie>

<http:www.familysearch.org/learn/wiki/en/Sheepeater_Indians>

<http:www.geocities.com/naforts/id.html>

<http:www.home.att.net/~mman/DoriansWife.htm>

<http:www.kstrom.net/isk/maps/Dakotas/sd.html>

<http:www.legendofamerica.com/na-bannock.html>

<http:www.legendsofamerica.com/id-forthall.html>

<http:www.legendsofAmerica.com/na-Shoshone.html>

<http:www.mountainmeadows.unl.edu/archive/mmm.news.nyt.18580204.ht ml>

<http:www.mountaintrappers.org/history/hudsons.htm>

<http:www.mt.pioneer.cm/archive-July-Sheepeater.htm>

<http:www.nps.gov/archive/fola/Laramie.htm>

<http:www.parksandrecreation.idaho.gov/parks/bear-lake>

<http:www.primitiveways.com/tule_ethnobotany.html>

<http:www.seidaho.org/forthall.html>

<http:www.shoshonebannocktribes.com/Shoshone-bannock-history. html>

<http:www.shoshoneindian.com/default.htm>

<http:www.thefurtrapper.com/historical_landmarks.htm>

<http:www.trailtribes.org/lemhi/whos-who.htm>

<http:www.washingtonwars.net/Ward%20Massacre.htm>

Author explores inside of a 19th century
stone house in southeastern Oregon.
About the Author

Born in Lexington, Nebraska, Robert Bolen, B.A. has a degree in Archeology/Anthropology. In an Archeology class, he was informed that because of his Mongolian eye-fold, he was part Indian. In 1755, a Bolen ancestor was taken captive by Delaware Indians and later rescued with her baby daughter, Robb's Great, Great, Grandmother. When rescued, the poor girl (just 17) was scalped, but she lived. A French scalp was the size of a silver dollar. Family says she combed her hair to hide the scar and lived to be well over one hundred years of age. Bolen's served under George Washington in the American Revolution. In 1777, the author's ancestors erected Fort Bolin, near Cross Creek, Pennsylvania for protection from Indian attacks. Two ancestors were killed in Kentucky by Shawnee Indians allied to the British. Great Grandad Gilbert Bolen rode with the Ohio Fourth Cavalry in the Civil War under General Sherman. In 1866, Gilbert brought his wife and six children west to Nebraska in a Conestoga wagon. Gran-dad Denver Colorado Bolen knew Buffalo Bill Cody in western Nebraska. Bolen is an authority on Indian artifacts and glass trade beads. Robb and Dori Bolen reside in Nampa, Idaho, near Boise. Robb owns the website, Fort Boise Bead Trader.com.

PHOTOGRAPHS
COURTESY OF
AZUSA Publishing, LLC
3575 S. Fox Street
Englewood, CO 80110

Email: azusa@azusapublishing.com

Phone Toll-free: 888-783-0077

Phone/Fax: 303-783-0073

BOOKS WRITTEN BY ROBERT BOLEN

Smoke Signals & Wagon Tracks

American Indian Tribes of Idaho

Blackfeet Raiders Nomads of the North

The Horse Indians

The Lakota Sioux Indians

The Medicine Crow Indians

War Chief Paulina
& His Renegade
Band of Paiutes

Graphic Design Services
provided by

DESIGNER

Cover Design

Book Layout

Text and Page Formatting

Editing

Photo Clarification and Enhancement

Etc.

Bonnie Fitzpatrick

208.249.2635

bjfitz777@msn.com

JERRY LEE YOUNG'S
IDAHO HERITAGE MUSEUM
2390 HWY. 93 SOUTH #B
TWIN FALLS, IDAHO 83301

CPSIA information can be obtained
at www.ICGtesting.com
Printed in the USA
FSOW02n0108300315
5996FS